# FROM THE FOREWORD

The Bible is a portrait-gallery. Down through its pages, from Adam walking the mists of the cooling earth to the last dreaming seer of Revelation, moves a deathless procession of the most interesting men and women in the history of the world. Here they are: good men and bad, noble women and low, cowards and heroes, saints and devils, martyrs, apostates and apostles. They run the gamut of character from Jesus to Jezebel. Some were great (Moses, Elijah, Jeremiah, Paul), and some were puny (Methuselah, Issachar, Ananias, Ham).

We have tried to paint them as they are, as God made them, as they are painted in the

*(Continued on next page)*

*(Continued from previous page)*
Book. Here is no camouflage, no hiding of the weak nor maudlin laudation for the strong. Neither are they draped in the grave-clothes of a dead theology: let the theologians bury the theologic dead! We have but tried to make them come alive again, to act out their great drama for our own day, to make them seem as close and real (as indeed they are!) as the men and women you will meet in your office, on the street, in the Temple, tomorrow.

# WHO'S WHO

# IN THE

# BIBLE

## 250 BIBLE BIOGRAPHIES

### FRANK S. MEAD

FAMILY LIBRARY                     NEW YORK

TO
# MOTHER
WHO, THRU THE HARD YEARS,
SMILED AND STOOD FAST
WHILE OTHERS
SMILED AND TURNED AWAY

*29282*

# WHO'S WHO IN THE BIBLE
(Formerly published under the title *250 Bible Biographies*)

FAMILY LIBRARY
Published by arrangement with Harper & Row, Publishers, Inc.

Family Library edition published July, 1973

ISBN 0-515-03106-2

Printed in the United States of America

FAMILY LIBRARY is published by Pyramid Publications
919 Third Avenue, New York, New York 10022, U.S.A.

# CONTENTS

Aaron, 49
Abel, 4
Abiathar, 90
Abigail, 86
Abijah, 114
Abimelech, 67
Abner, 91
Abraham, 18
Absalom, 99
Achan, 59
Achsah, 54
Adah, 6
Adam, 1
Adonijah, 106
Adoniram, 113
Agrippa, 244
Ahab, 120
Ahasuerus, 157
Ahaz, 139
Ahijah, 110
Ahimelech, 88
Ahithophel, 100
Amasa, 102
Amaziah, 133
Amos, 169
Ananias, 230
Andrew, 194
Anna, 193
Annas, 220
Asa, 115
Asher, 39
Ashtoreth, 66
Athaliah, 127

Baal, 65
Baasha, 116
Balaam, 57
Balak, 56
Barabbas, 224
Barak, 61
Barnabas, 229
Bartimaeus, 216
Baruch, 178
Bath-Sheba, 97
Belshazzar, 151
Benaiah, 104
Benjamin, 43
Bildad, 166

Boaz, 76

Caiaphas, 221
Cain, 3
Caleb, 53
Chedorlaomer, 19
Chloe, 246
Claudia Procula,
 223
Cyrus, 153

Dan, 36
Daniel, 180
Darius, 152
David, 83
Deborah, 63
Delilah, 72
Demas, 248
Demetrius, 241
Diana, 240
Dionysius, 238
Doeg, 89
Dorcas, 234

Ehud, 60
Eldad, 52
Eli, 78
Elihu, 168
Elijah, 122
Eliphaz, 165
Elisha, 123
Elizabeth, 187
Enoch, 10
Enos, 9
Esau, 27
Esther, 163
Eve, 2
Ezekiel, 179
Ezra, 156

Felix, 242
Festus, 243

Gaal, 69
Gad, 38
Gamaliel, 232
Gideon, 64
Goliath, 82

Habakkuk, 175

Hagar, 21
Haggai, 181
Ham, 13
Haman, 161
Hannah, 77
Hezekiah, 141
Hiram, 105
Hosea, 170
Hoshea, 140
Hur, 50

Isaac, 24
Isaiah, 171
Ish-bosheth, 93
Ishmael, 22
Issachar, 40

Jacob, 28
Jael, 62
James, Brother of
 Jesus, 210
James, son of
 Alpheus, 203
James, son of
 Zebedee, 199
Japheth, 14
Jehoahaz of Israel,
 131
Jehoiachin, 147
Jehoiada, 129
Jehoiakim, 146
Jehoram of Israel,
 124
Jehoram of Judah,
 125
Jehoshaphat, 117
Jehu, 126
Jephthah, 70
Jeremiah, 177
Jeroboam the First,
 111
Jeroboam the
 Second, 134
Jesus, 191
Jezebel, 121
Joab, 92
Joanna, 208
Joash of Israel, 132

Joash of Judah, 130
Job, 164
Jochebed, 45
Joel, 183
John the Apostle, 200
John the Baptist, 188
Jonah, 184
Jonathan, 87
Joseph, 42
Joseph of Arimathea, 226
Joseph of Nazareth, 189
Joses, 209
Joshua, 51
Josiah, 145
Jotham, son of Jerubbaal, 68
Jotham, son of Uzziah, 136
Judah, 35
Judas Iscariot, 206
Jude, 211

Korah, 55

Laban, 26
Lamech, 5
Lazarus of Bethany, 215
Lazarus the Beggar, 214
Leah, 30
Levi, 34
Lot, 17
Luke, 227
Lydia, 237

Malachi, 185
Malchus, 218
Manasseh, 143
Mark, 219
Martha, 212
Mary Magdalene, 207
Mary of Bethany, 213

Mary of Nazareth, 190
Matthew, 201
Matthias, 228
Melchizedek, 20
Memucan, 159
Mephibosheth, 95
Merab, 84
Methuselah, 11
Micah, 172
Michal, 85
Miriam, 48
Moloch, 144
Mordecai, 160
Moses, 47

Naaman, 128
Nahum, 173
Naomi, 73
Naphthali, 37
Nathan, 98
Nathanael, 197
Nebuchadnezzar, 149
Nehemiah, 155
Nicodemus, 198
Noah, 12

Obadiah, 176
Omri, 119
Onesimus, 250
Orpah, 74

Paul, 233
Pekah, 137
Peter, 195
Philetus, 249
Philip, 196
Phoebe, 245
Pilate, 222
Priscilla, 239
Pul, 138

Queen of Sheba, 108

Rachel, 29
Rahab, 58
Rebekah, 25
Reuben, 32
Rezon, 109
Rehoboam, 112

Rizpah, 103
Ruth, 75

Samson, 71
Samuel, 79
Sarah, 23
Saul, 80
Sennacherib, 142
Seth, 8
Shadrach, 150
Shem, 15
Shimei, 101
Shiphrah, 44
Silas, 235
Simon of Cyrene, 225
Simon Zelotes, 204
Simeon, of Jerusalem, 192
Simeon, son of Jacob, 33
Solomon, 107
Stephen, 231

Terah, 16
Thaddeus, 205
Thermouthis, 46
Thomas, 202
Timothy, 236
Titus, 247

Uriah, 96
Uzzah, 94
Uzziah, 135

Vashti, 158

Witch of Endor, 81

Zaccheus, 217
Zacharias, 186
Zebulun, 41
Zechariah, 182
Zedekiah, 148
Zephaniah, 174
Zeresh, 162
Zerubbabel, 154
Zillah, 7
Zilpah, 31
Zimri, 118
Zophar, 167

# *Adam*

EASTWARD IN EDEN LIVED ADAM, ALONE. THE "FIRST man," set down in a rapturous earthly paradise. He had the body of an Apollo Belvedere, the mind and heart of an innocent child. In his blood were saints and devils; he was the fountain-head of a long heredity. Clothed in the tapestry of legend, obscure in the labyrinths of folk-lore, he is the most challenged figure in the great portrait-gallery of the Book. Yet, ridiculed or accepted, he is your portrait, mine.

Strangely formed of divinity and dust, he gave to us the two basic elements of our natures: the materialistic dust of which our bodies are made, the breath of the Father to give life, meaning, vision to our clay.

Just how or where the Creator molded him is uncertain—and unimportant. What *is* important here is the evidence of the molding process from Adam to Jesus. The child-man in Eden, faced with his own silly sin, could whimper weakly, "The woman . . . she gave me of the tree. . . ." But the ultimate Man in Gethsemane, sinless and offering himself for the sin of others, could cry triumphantly, ". . . nevertheless, not my will, but thine, be done."

*Genesis 2:7 ff.; 3:12.*

1

# Eve

Sent to be co-wanderer in the mists of the cooling earth was Eve, wife of Adam. We harshly call her weak, the agent through whom the first man fell. Weak she may have been; foolish she certainly was. More keen to the garden's glories than her mate, she sought to enjoy them more by gaining greater wisdom and understanding, hoping thereby that she and hers might "be like gods." She was wrong in preferring the power of a transient wisdom to the power of an abiding love. She coveted a trifle and she lost a paradise. But that is only half her story. It is only what Eve was within the garden.

Outside the garden she reared a family, ruled a nursery which was the cradle of nations, the training-school of kings. She bore lusty Cain, weak Abel, Seth, the head of the line of Jesus Christ. The selfish, lazy greeds of Eden have left her completely as she cries now, "I have gotten a man from the Lord." She went unquestioning with Adam out into the deep wilderness, in passive endurance and silent fortitude, there to become the perfect type of patient motherhood.

*Genesis 2:18 ff.; 3:1 ff.; 4:1 f., 25.*

# Cain

CAIN WAS THE FIRST CHILD OF THE FIRST MAN AND
woman, the first farmer and first murderer. In him war
was born. Jealous of his shepherd-brother Abel, whose
sacrifice seemed more acceptable to God than his own,
he lured him to a lonely, open field and struck him
dead. God set a mark on Cain and the tribe of Cain to
protect him, and them, from the vengeance of men.
God is always more merciful than men.

Cain the Killer took to his heels, but his heels were
slow. Guilt, God, and conscience chased him fast, and a
voice kept whispering, ". . . the voice of thy brother's
blood crieth unto me from the ground."

He built a city, founded a dynasty, fathered the tribe
which still forges the weapons of war. He left some les-
sons we have not yet learned: that violence brings its
own violent reward, that each man *is* his brother's
keeper. Cain learned that, but have we? The graves of
ten million dead in Flanders fields cry out to us, ". . .
the voice of thy brother's blood crieth unto me from the
ground. . . ." But . . .

*Genesis 4:1.*

3

# *Abel*

GENTLE ABEL, THOUGH THE BREATH OF THE FATHER was so strong within him, was no match for furious Cain. He went down easily, in the prime of his days. Cain left descendants and the record of a brute masculine strength. Even Byron praised him, to the tune of Europe's cheers. But what of frail Abel? What could he leave? His very name means "breath," "vapor," "vanity."

He left far more than Cain. He bequeathed unwittingly a spirit that has proved invaluable in tempering the cruelties of the sons of Cain. He left the conviction that the worth of sacrifice depends not at all upon the nature of the offering, but upon the character of the offerer. Faint faith gets but a faint reward. Even Jesus mentions Abel, calls him the first martyr. He created faith out of spilled blood. By faith he, being dead, yet speaketh. Speaketh in Abraham, Moses, the Prophets, Calvary.

*Genesis 4:2; Matt. 23:35.*

# Lamech

THE CURSED STRAIN IN CAIN'S BLOOD RAN SWIFT AND hot in the veins of antediluvian men. In Lamech, his lineal descendant, it reached a boiling-point. Lamech is the first polygamist: he had two famous wives, Adah and Zillah. And he had three famous sons: Jubal, Jabal, Tubal-Cain. He uttered the first Biblical poetry. It might have been beautiful. It was horrible. Listen to him singing to his wives as he returns from battle:

> "Adah and Zillah, hear my voice;
> Wives of Lamech, hearken unto my speech;
> A man I slay for wounding me,
> Yea, a youth for bruising me.
> If Cain be avenged sevenfold,
> Lamech shall be seventy and seven."

They were a fierce lot, killing a man for a wound, a boy for a mere blow. Ten times as bloodthirsty as Cain, and proud of it. Murder was in their blood, vengeance became with them a tribal affair; they covered the earth with their red stain. Moral corruption and degeneracy grew apace. Only a flood could stop it.

*Genesis 4:19.*

# *Adah*

WHY DID LAMECH MARRY ADAH? HE WAS CRUDE AND marble-hearted, she a lambent flame of beauty in the deep antediluvian night. Adah surely was dark-eyed and a dreamer, for in her two sons she cradled two noble, dreaming arts.

One son she named Jabal; he was the father of herdsmen, of cattlemen and shepherds, of all "such as dwell in tents." He knew the singing, swinging glory of the stars as he watched his flocks by night; he could interpret the great symphonies the winds sing as they rustle the leaves of a tree.

Close to his side grew Jubal, also Adah's son. He too knew the stars and the wind's singing. He knew them even better, put them to a finer use than Jabal. He was "father of all such as handle the harp and organ." Like Pan, he coaxed music from a reed plucked by the river; he lured tunes from a harp of cornstalk strings.

Adah cradled the arts. Her name means "light," or "dawn."

# *Zillah*

LAMECH'S HOUSE KNEW SHADOW AS WELL AS LIGHT: Zillah's name means "shade." Adah was the Mary of this early home, and Zillah was its Martha. She was practical, with many irons in the fire and little time for dreams. Yet she too cradled art. Like her sister, she had two children: the girl Naamah, of whom we know nothing, and the boy Tubal-Cain, "an instructor of every artificer in brass and iron." In other words, the father of smiths. A teaching craftsman. Practical son of a practical mother, he forged spears and swords as well as bowls and candlesticks.

An old legend says that this Tubal-Cain made for his father Lamech a sturdy iron-tipped arrow, and that Lamech, hunting in the dark forest, drove the deadly shaft through the breast of old, wandering, fugitive Cain. A legend, perhaps, but altogether possible. The grisly instruments of Tubal-Cain and the ghastly blundering of Lamech are still part and parcel of our lives. Brother faced brother and son faced father at Antietam and the Marne.

There is still shadow to balance light.

*Genesis 4:22.*

7

# Seth

MOTHER EVE MUST OFTEN HAVE WEPT OVER HER CHILdren. Abel was dead, Cain was a renegade. It was not until Adam was one hundred and thirty years old that fresh hope and joy came to her. Seth was born. Now she does not rejoice in "a strong man from the Lord"; now it is ". . . God . . . hath appointed me another seed instead of Abel, whom Cain slew." Seth ("appointed" or "substituted") came to do the work which Abel should have done. He came to father a line as good as Cain's was bad. The unholy seed of the fratricide was not to rule the world alone. With it was to grow the seed of Seth, its righteous counterpart.

In Seth's line were the Men Who Walked with God: Enos, Enoch, Noah, Jesus. To them were intrusted faith and mercy; they were as plainly marked the children of God as Cain's clan were marked the children of sin.

Like two mighty armies they have struggled through the ages, the earth their battle-ground, their prize the souls of men.

Like two mighty rivers their blood streams flow, the one polluting and poisoning, the other cleansing and purifying.

*Genesis 4:25 f.; 5:5 ff.*

# *Enos*

~~~~~~~~~~~~~~~~~~~~~~~~~~~~~~~~~~~~~~

SOME CALL HIM ENOSH. HE HAS TWO CLAIMS TO IM-
mortality. One is that as the worthy son of Seth he was
a strong link in an indispensable genealogical chain.
The other is that somehow, in his day, "men began to
call on the name of the Lord." Being a mere biological
link is not much of a calling. It is more of an accident.
But to be the medium through whom one's fellow-men
come to think of God as personal—that is glorious!

Enos may have been an early priest. We like to think
that he was. Or he may have been just one of a group of
laymen who through meditation and prayer got hold of
a new way of thinking about God. Either way, he is ep-
ochal. He represents the day when enlightened men
crossed the line from primitive superstition to the worship of a God who was not a wraith in a column of
smoke, nor a dumb spirit in a rock, nor a breeze sighing
in a tree. God was real. He had a name. It was Jehovah.

*Genesis 4:26.*

# Enoch

ENOCH, SON OF JARED AND FATHER OF METHUSELAH, flashes like a streak of sharp clean lightning across the lowering, evil skies that announce the flood. The most commanding figure from Eden to Ararat, he "walked with God" in a world made hideous by the screams of murdered men, repulsive as a jubilee-house of crime. In the midst of the din, Enoch communed. In everything he thought of God. To his fellows he was a type of perfected humanity; to posterity he is known as The Man Who Could Not Die.

Here, in the days of the beginnings, æons before the Christ, dawns the hope of immortality. Enoch never knew death. He was "translated," like Elijah, from one phase of existence to another. "God took him." His life never stopped. It simply went on. It was not resuscitated nor even resurrected. It was eternal. He always thought of it that way. Life and God for him were always in the present tense.

Why is it not so with us?

*Genesis 5:18 ff.*

# *Methuselah*

MARK TWAIN ONCE MADE A COMMENCEMENT ADDRESS which he opened with these words: "The subject of my remarks is Methuselah; he lived to be nine hundred and sixty-nine years; but what of that? There was nothing doing." The great humorist did well: he put into those few terse words the complete biography of the Bible's most useless man. What a record for the son of an Enoch!

To Methuselah, evidently, life was just one day after another. He holds the record for birthdays and for nothing else. His life had length but no breadth, no depth. No vision ever glorified *his* clay. His heart never leaped at the sight of a rainbow in the sky, his leaden feet never took him walking with his father's God. He just existed for nine hundred and sixty-nine years, of the earth earthy. Then—"he died."

Why must our Methuselahs live at all?

*Genesis 5:21 ff.*

# Noah

THE GRANDSON OF METHUSELAH IS THE LEGENDARY Second Father of Mankind. His name is Noah, and his life is in three parts.

His first five centuries are a total blank. He was growing in body, mind and soul.

At five hundred three sons came, Shem, Ham, Japheth, to live surrounded by men who were fallen angels, demons in human form, Satans and Jezebels, pitiless, defiant, strong. "There were giants in the earth in those days." Among them Noah, like Enoch, moved with the Almighty. He feared God and helped men. St. Peter calls him "a preacher of righteousness." When Jehovah resolved to destroy the giants and the giant evil of the world, he set this righteous man to building his Brobdingnagian ark. In went the animals, two by two. When Noah was six hundred years old, the Flood came. When it was over, he led his family ashore and built the first Biblical altar, offered the first burnt sacrifice.

He lived after the Flood three hundred fifty years, and he died.

Forget the ark and the animals. Remember that righteousness delivers men and nations, that God is One, that sin pays off in death.

*Genesis 5:32-9:29.*

# Ham

HARDLY HAD THE SMOKE OF THE FIRST SACRIFICE
blown off in the fresh clean sky when the Second Father
fell. Not as guilty Adam fell, but innocently. Noah
drank too much wine and fell into a drunken sleep.
Think twice before you laugh at him: Ham failed to,
and regretted it. This drunkenness was due not to delib-
erate excess; it was the accidental discovery of the
power of the juice of the grape. Ham saw his father
drunk and burst into uproarious laughter. Men drunk
are always a great joke—and a great tragedy. Unadul-
terated tragedy, for Ham.

When Noah awoke and the fumes left his brain, he
wrathfully uttered a fearful curse upon the offspring of
Ham: "Cursed be Canaan; a servant of servants shall he
be." Ham is supposed to have become the ancestor,
therefore, of three great groups of "servants"—Egyptians, Canaanites, and Ethiopians.

"Servants" is a misleading appellation. Considering
the world-rulers born within the ranks of the sons of
Ham, considering Egyptian architecture and the Negro
spiritual, they seem to be something more.

*Genesis 9:20 ff.; 10:6 ff.*

13

# Japheth

THESE MEN BETWEEN NOAH AND ABRAHAM ARE THE "fathers" of races, tribes, and peoples. We must think of them as representing the great "powers" of the earth contemporary with early Israel.

Ham's brothers, Shem and Japheth, saw nothing funny in their father's disgrace. They were ashamed of him, for him. They covered him with a robe, and nursed him back to sobriety. For that Noah was grateful; he was as magnanimous in rewarding them as he had been stern in cursing Ham.

"God," he said, "shall enlarge Japheth, and he shall dwell in the tents of Shem; and Canaan shall be his servant." Thus, say the historians, Japheth and his heirs became the northern nations, the dwellers in "the isles of the Gentiles." That is, they inhabited the coasts of the Mediterranean Sea in Europe and Asia Minor. It is the second great division of the post-deluge world.

Certainly, the sons of Japheth have ruled over the sons of Ham. Is that because of the prophecy of Father Noah? Or is it because the "westward" nations, following Christ (descended from Noah), have practiced more faithfully the kindly philosophy of Japheth?

*Genesis 9:20 ff.; 10:2 ff.*

# *Shem*

SHEM, THE THIRD OF THE TRIO, WENT WITH JAPETH TO help the fallen father, and reaped a rich reward for his act of love. He was made ancestor to the Hebrews (who claim to have sprung from Shem's third son, Arphaxad). Modern scholars give the name Shemitic, or *Semitic,* to the tongue spoken by his descendants. The record of the Bible, from now on, is the record of his people.

Father Noah went even farther than this in honoring dutiful Shem. He set an especial blessing on his tribe: "Blessed be the Lord [the] God of Shem." His issue were to be not only "Israelites." They were to be the Chosen People of the One True God. It is the divine commission.

Israel is a nation set apart, after the blessing of Noah on Shem, for a holy purpose among all the peoples of the earth. The heirs of Ham and Japeth might spend themselves in wars for empire, but the children of Shem were to be concerned with a kingdom not made with hands, but eternal, in the heavens.

*Genesis 9:20 ff.; 10:21 ff.*

# *Terah*

TERAH SEEMS MORE REAL, MORE HUMAN, THAN THESE last ones, and his story, also real and human, is quaintly believable. We might pass him by with simply saying that he sired the great Israelite, Ishmaelite, Midianite, Moabite, Ammonite tribes. But here is the human Terah:

For a hundred years he had been a shepherd, sitting with his flocks on the hillsides of Ur, of the Chaldees. He was gentle, reverent, devout, as all Chaldeans were; he was an idol-worshiper, as all Chaldeans were. He grew old and his sons grew up, taking over the care of the sheep while the father rested and dreamed of yesterday.

One day the shepherd wanderlust got hold of him and he decided, abruptly, to seek new pastures. Down the road he went, toward Canaan, tottering, slower and slower. At last he died—on the road. An old idolater, on a strange road, with his hurrying sons. Ahead, on the trail, fame and glory beckoned for them. But the old man never knew. They buried him at Haran.

At the grave stood his son Abraham, and a young grandson, called Lot.

# Lot

TOGETHER SON AND GRANDSON WENT ON TO CANAAN, to Egypt when famine came. Driven thence, they came back to Bethel, where their flocks multiplied so rapidly that they deemed it wise to separate and go their separate ways. Lot, given his choice of a homestead, looked at the well-watered, green Jordan Valley and said, "I'll take that." It was typical of him. Lot was a business man, an opportunist, an Oriental bargainer, a man of the world.

But it was a bad choice. War was in that valley. Caught between the hostile forces, Lot was taken prisoner and freed again—by Abraham! He married a woman of Sodom, the wickedest city in man's literature. Hopelessly corrupt, God burned it to the ground, letting only Lot and his family escape. Lot's wife looked back. Pity her. Lot lost only his house. She was losing her home, her neighbors, her friends.

Lot's last act was one of incest. From his daughters came the nations of Ammon, Moab.

Lot grasped, and his grasping brought him woe. He was short on character; he was "righteous" only in comparison with the men of Sodom. And that is not saying very much.

*Genesis 11:31-14:16; 19:1 ff.; II Peter 2:7, 8.*

# *Abraham*

HAVE YOU SEEN THE MATTERHORN? HERE IS THE MAT-
terhorn of Bibical humanity. Abraham dominates them
all. Next to Jesus, he is the noblest spirit that ever wore
the flesh of man.

Contemporaries called him the Friend of God: in
him is our first clear vision of the Father. With him religion advances: human sacrifice was disapproved, and
monotheism begun. The followers of three great religions call him Progenitor: Christians, Jews, Moham-
medans. The very air he breathed was filled with faith.

By faith, at God's command, he led the way through
the wilderness, confident that God was to make him the
father of a great new nation. By faith he lifted his knife
to slay his son; God accepted his obedience and stopped
the hand before it struck. Faith made him the pioneer
of civilization, the founder of an empire for God and
righteousness.

He had a massive physique (like Michelangelo's
"Moses") and a majestic mind. Self-possessed and self-
sacrificing, courageous, generous, meek, patient, and
sensible, he is the worthy father of Israel and patriarch
of the Church, a man of destiny plotting a great destiny
for a great people.

Father Abraham!

*Genesis 11:27-25:11; II Chronicles 20:7;*
*James 2:23.*

# Chedorlaomer

CHEDORLAOMER WAS THE FIGHTING BARBARIAN, KING of Elam, who upset the plans of greedy Lot. He was a military scourge; he swept north, east, south, and west with a fury like Attila's; he dreamed, like Alexander, of conquering the world. A handful of fighting shepherds broke his dream.

He had conquered the Jordan plain some years before, but, absent on the business of another war, five Canaanite kings rebelled and dared him to come on. He came. Leading a confederacy of Messopotamian kings, he met the rebels in the vale of Siddim. The battle of the kings! The old barbarian won, put Sodom and Gomorrah to the torch, turned northward with his spoils—with poor Lot a prisoner.

Halfway home, a rabble army of shepherds, led by an aroused Abraham, ambushed them, threw them into rout, nearly destroyed them all; like Gideon surprising the Midianites, or the farmers behind the stone walls of Lexington.

So passed Chedorlaomer, a first-class fighting-man. Abraham's character never appeared to better advantage than in this victory: it was masterful, complete, one of the decisive battles of the world. The spoils of Chedorlaomer were his. He refused them.

*Genesis 14:1 ff.*

# Melchizedek

MEET THE MOST TANTALIZING MAN IN THE BIBLE: WE know just enough about him to want to know more, and more we shall never know. Melchizedek was "without father, without mother, without descent, having neither beginning of days nor end of life, but made like unto the Son of God; abideth a priest continually." A weird human meteor who flashes briefly across history's firmament and is quickly gone.

He was the king of Salem (Jerusalem?) and he was more: the first priest, and a magnificent one. He worshiped God stubbornly in a day of swift decline, gave to Him a ministry so noble, so exalted, as to be the model for the Christ's. For Christ, says the author of Hebrews, was "a priest forever after the order of Melchizedek."

The perfect minister! It is one thing to preach and pray in comfortable surroundings, where listeners easily agree; it is quite another to preach and pray in the face of opposition or disheartening carelessness.

Abraham, returning home from the battle with Chedorlaomer, met Melchizedek and was blessed by him. Like ships that pass in the night: the father of Israel's faith, and the greatest preacher of it.

*Genesis 14:18 ff.*

# Hagar

HAGAR WAS A SLAVE, PURCHASED IN EGYPT TO SERVE AS
maid to Abraham's wife. Catastrophe was her lot, dealt
from a quick and unseen hand. Abraham and Sarah,
growing old and fearful lest there should be no son to
carry on the line, agree that Abraham shall have an heir
through the Egyptian slave. Hagar conceives, and poor
Sarah, chagrined and jealous, torments the expectant
mother until she flees into the wilderness. But "an angel
of the Lord" stops her flight, sends her back, and Ishmael is born. Immediately Hagar is transformed; no
longer is she the meek, submissive slave. She is arrogant, boastful, vaunting her triumph constantly before
the eyes of the luckless wife.

The fate dealt again—God sent a son to *Sarah*. He is
weak. Ishmael is strong. Trouble brews; quarrels between the mothers make the home a bedlam. Two
women quarreling, two children listening.

At last Hagar is driven into the desert with her child.
Across the burning sands she wanders; miraculously,
she reaches the Nile. There she dies.

In her mother-love Hagar is heroic, but in her weak
character and effrontery she is a piteous puppet of
tragedy.

*Genesis 16:1 ff.; 21:8 ff.*

# Ishmael

ISHMAEL RAN THE GAMUT FROM PROSPERITY TO DE-
spair. Born the heir of a great house and rich, he was
untamable, quick as a hawk, insolent as an ingrate.
"Sarah saw the son of Hagar . . . mocking." That is,
making life miserable for her gentle Isaac. Disinherited,
he went with his distracted mother across the desert,
married at her request a girl of Egypt. A dutiful son was
Ishmael, carrying the taint of the mother's spirit in his
blood, the bitter memory of her sufferings in his mind.
Like mother, like son. As the boy grew, so the man. He
and his sons were as wild asses, a tribe of archers,
fighters, their hands lifted against all men, warlike, forever unsubdued. In Bible days they were called Ishmaelites; in modern days we call them Arabs, or Bedouins.
Still untamed, and wild as desert wind, they are the enemies of peace and progress, the most formidable oppo-
nents Christianity has ever had. Under the banners of
Mohammed they curdled the blood of Christian Europe
with the cry, "Death to the infidels."

Might history have taken another course, we wonder, if Ishmael had been the son of Sarah, and not of
Hagar?

*Genesis 16:4 ff.; 17:18 ff.; 21:8 ff.; 25:12 ff.*

# Sarah

ABRAHAM MARRIED WELL. THE GIRL HE CHOSE WAS
Sarah, who had enough of beauty to make a Pharaoh
covet her, enough of courage to stay at her husband's
side while he struggled to build a new home in a new
country. She was the mother of Isaac, alternately cruel
and lovely, radiant and repulsive, lovely princess and
despotic queen.

In conjugal obedience and loyalty she is unsurpassed.
She is one of the few people in Scripture who laughed
(when told that she, an old woman, should yet bear a
son)! Yet when Isaac came, she championed him, defended him as a tigress defends her cub. She spent her
life in sacrifice for Abraham and Isaac.

Sarah only wanted to defend her fireside from the
dark shadow of polygamous love, her son from the loss
of his birthright. She could not bring herself to share
her love for Abraham with an Egyptian servant. She
struggled to keep unsullied her marriage vow; she loved
not wisely but well. Her shortcomings were typical of
her day; her virtues are an example for womankind forever.

*Genesis 12:1 ff.; 17:15 ff.; 18:1 ff.; 21:1 ff.;
23:1 ff.*

# Isaac

As a boy Sarah's son was dreamy, romantic, contemplative; as a youth he was a philosopher, a devout religionist lacking the energy and strong character of his father, Abraham. In old age he was senile, pathetic, blind, and childish. His name, ironically means, "laughter." His life held laughter; not the laughter of a dog with a bone nor of a man with bursting barns, but the laughter of hard sacrifice rewarded.

He did not weep or struggle when his father made ready to sacrifice him on Mount Moriah. He went gladly. He understood. He obeyed, surrendering himself to God.

His youth he sacrificed to digging wells for water, wells his father had dug and the Philistines destroyed. For his father's memory he did that, and to slack his children's thirst. His self-denying love of peace caused him the loss of many a well to the Philistines and the servants of Abimelech. He hated war, loved peace. Aged, his son Jacob tricked him. But even that he called the will of God.

His life of outward sacrifice brought him an inward peace. While Ishmael was conquering the kingdoms of the earth, Isaac was gaining the kingdom of heaven.

*Genesis 21:1 ff.; 22:1 ff.; 24; 25:5-28:9; 35:27 ff.*

# Rebekah

REBEKAH SAT BY A WELL IN UR; A CARAVAN STOPPED, and Eliezer, servant of Abraham, asked for a drink of water. He also asked her to return with him and marry Isaac, lonely and brooding over his mother's death. Would she go? She went. Partly selfish, that. She knew she was marrying money. Rebekah was beautiful, vivacious, calculating.

Yet she was a good wife. She comforted Isaac, dispelled his loneliness, and he came to love her well enough to lie about her, to protect her, in exactly the same manner that Abraham had once lied about Sarah. She gave Isaac two sons—Jacob, Esau.

She loved them both, but Jacob was her pet. She tricked her aged husband into giving him the parental blessing which belonged to Esau. Isaac must have hated her for that. Esau raged. Rebekah repented, bundled Jacob off to live for a little while with Laban, till the storm blew over.

She never saw him again.

She loved too narrowly. She was shrewd, tactful, unscrupulous, cruel. She is less lovely than Hagar. She died frustrated, heckled, embittered.

*Genesis 24:15 ff.; 25:19 ff.; 26:6 ff.; 27:1-28:5.*

25

# *Laban*

HAD SHAKESPEARE LIVED IN CANAAN, HE SURELY
would have named Laban his "Shylock." Laban out-Shy-
locked Shylock: one pound of flesh was never enough
for him.

When his sister Rebekah was asked to marry Isaac,
his miser-heart leaped for joy. He had seen the jewels of
the caravan at the well; the camel-bells sang to him a
sweet song of easy wealth.

When nephew Jacob arrived, his eyes sparkled. Here
was a strong young man and rich, marriageable, desir-
able, and Laban with two marriageable daughters under
his roof! He tricked Jacob into fourteen years' hard
labor, with the daughters as the prize. Six years more he
took from the lad's life, but he was outsmarted in the
end. Jacob watched his chance, took flight one day with
the best of the flocks, the household gods, and the two
daughters! Laban, by forced marches, caught up with
him in Mount Gilead. There they wrangled, signed a
truce, promised never again to bother one another. And
be it said for Laban that he never broke his vow.

He was sharp, unprincipled, a knave. But can you
read his story without a chuckle?

*Genesis 24:28 ff.; 29:13-31:55.*

26

# *Esau*

ESAU, ELDEST SON OF ISAAC, CAME IN FROM HUNTING, tired and hungry. "Feed me," he shouts at Jacob. Jacob did—in exchange for Esau's birthright. Birthrights meant little to Esau. He thought more of his stomach than of his soul. He was thoughtless, impetuous, loving a good time. He had all the gay, whistling picturesqueness of a cheerful tramp.

He broke his father's heart by marrying Hittite women, thereby allying himself with idolatry and Godlessness. Yet, heedless and capricious as he was, his father idolized him, loved him in spite of his faults. That is fatherhood *par excellence*.

Esau and Jacob, after the theft of the blessing, kept out of each other's way. They remained in enmity even when, after twenty years, on Jacob's return from exile, Esau, *à la* prodigal son, ran "to meet him and embraced him, and fell on his neck, and kissed him; and they wept."

Years later they stood together when their father's body was entombed.

In the brothers' warfare is symbolized the struggle between Edom and Israel; in Esau's repudiation of things spiritual for things material is seen the root of human sin.

Odd, with Esau's example, that men still prefer a ball game to an hour of prayer!

*Genesis 25:27 ff.; 26:34 ff.; 27:1 ff.; 33:4; 35:28.*

# *Jacob*

IF LABAN BE SCRIPTURE'S SHYLOCK, THEN JACOB IS ITS Dr. Jekyll and Mr. Hyde. His life is one long struggle between two natures, one base and the other divine.

As a youth he was a cheat. He cheated Esau, Laban, his own father. Yet even as he cheated he was struggling to be better. Fleeing to Laban's house, that first long night away from home, he dreamed of angels going *up* and *down* a ladder:

> Yet, in my dreams I'd be
> Nearer, my God, to thee.

Even as he matched wits with Laban he was serving years of torture for the girl he loved. ". . . and they seemed unto him but a few days, for the love he had for her."

He might have died a trickster, but for one night at Peniel when he faced God fairly and fought his problem through. That wrestling in the dark was the turning-point of his life; thereafter, having given God command over his life, he was a new man, a Prince of God. God changed his name, then, to Israel.

He had much property, little happiness.

His twelve sons were the twelve tribes of Israel. Israel, too, struggled with God.

*Genesis 25:27; 27:18 ff.; 28:10 ff.;*
*20:21 ff.; 32:24 ff.*

28

# Rachel

RACHEL, LIKE REBEKAH, MET HER LOVER AT A DESERT well. It was love at first sight. It remained love, beautifully, to the end.

This wife of Jacob's was "beautiful and well favored." Gracious. Kindly. Patient. She saw her lover tricked into marriage with her sister Leah, yet she waited gladly her long years to share his love. She was childless, a curse and a sorrow in the East, while Leah gave son after son to Jacob. She wanted a child desperately. "Give me children, or else I die." Yet she never turned bitter, like Sarah before her. Finally Joseph came to her.

When Jacob ran from Laban, Rachel stole the images of the household gods, and hid them cleverly when Laban searched their tents. Forgive her; she loved her friendly fireside gods. Incidentally, Laban had trained her, himself, in his own school of deceit.

She died giving birth to Benjamin, in a jostling caravan, in the middle of a long journey. Her second boy, and she had to die! Broken-hearted, Jacob buried her at the side of the road, within a mile of the little town of Bethlehem.

*Genesis 29:17 ff.; 30:1, 22 ff.; 31:19; 35:16 ff.*

# *Leah*

RACHEL MOURNED HER CHILDLESSNESS, BUT EXULTED in Jacob's love. Leah gave her husband sons, but mourned because she never gained his love. She loved Jacob with a secret, passionate calm, but he never reciprocated. She was never more than tolerated. Perhaps her mate thought her as guilty as Laban in the trick at the altar. At any rate, she was unsought and unloved. She had a blemish, a cast in her eyes that disfigured her.

Have you read that scene in Tennyson's "Guinevere" in which Arthur speaks to his groveling queen?

> "I cannot touch thy lips, they are not mine,
> But Lancelot's: nay, they never were the King's."

Jacob's lips, Jacob's heart were never Leah's. They were Rachel's.

Leah's children were Reuben, Simeon, Levi, Judah, Issachar, Zebulun, and Dinah. But Jacob's favorites were the children of Rachel, Joseph and Benjamin.

Leah lies buried in the family tomb, the Cave of Machpelah. There also lay Abraham and Sarah, Isaac and Rebekah; soon Jacob was to join them there in death.

Do they love each other more, we wonder, beyond the grave?

*Genesis 29:17 ff.; 30:18 ff.; 49:31.*

# *Zilpah*

ZILPAH WAS JACOB'S CONCUBINE. SHE HAD BEEN GIVEN to Leah by Laban to serve as an attendant, and she had been passed on from Leah to Jacob, as one would pass on sheep or furniture. Leah, wife and lover of Jacob, rejoiced in Zilpah's sons! She called them Gad (fortune) and Asher (happy). It is a system of marriage and marriage morals hard for us to understand.

There was nothing particularly shameful in being a concubine, nor was there any great difference in station between the children of wives and concubines, as there is today. All the sons of Jacob were tribal leaders. But the wife enjoyed one privilege the concubine never had. She could not be cut off from her husband without a bill of divorce. The concubines could be dropped at a moment's notice.

They were sometimes Hebrew girls sold by their fathers, sometimes Gentiles captured in war, sometimes foreigners purchased abroad, sometimes Canaanitish women. They all had a precarious, thankless existence. They could expect no love. They were pawns, played cruelly by primitive men, swept quickly off the board to give a larger piece free play.

*Genesis 29:24; 30:9.*

# Reuben

REUBEN HAD ALL THE ADVANTAGES OF A PETTED, FIRST-born child. He threw them easily away. Impetuous as Esau, unbalanced as Ishmael, he had an affair with Bilhah, one of his father's concubines, which turned the father's blessing into a curse. A moment's madness. A spotted character.

It was an unhappy mistake, for at heart Reuben was a nobleman. When his brothers plotted to kill Joseph, he saved the lad's life by suggesting the pit. When he found the pit empty and Joseph headed for Egypt, he rent his clothes and wept. Again, pleading with his father to let young Benjamin go to the Egyptian court, he cried, "Slay my two sons if I bring him not [back] to thee." Ardent. Generous. Ruled by love and compassion. But for that one mad hour with Bilhah. . . .

His tribe was inferior. It produced no great hero, judge, or prophet. The Reubenites clung to their flocks in the green pastures east of Jordan, between the Arnon and Gilead. They disliked war. Like their founder, their opportunities were legion, their fruits poor.

That was not Reuben's fault, but theirs.

*Genesis 29:32; 35:22; 37:18 ff.; 42:36 ff.; 49:3 f.; Numbers 32:1 ff.*

# *Simeon*

SIMEON, LEAH'S SECOND SON AND BROTHER TO REUBEN, was not like Reuben at all. He was pugnacious. He loved a fight. He and his tribe spent most of their time fighting.

Simeon isn't mentioned very often. In fact, only twice. Once he joined hands with Levi in a massacre which Jacob, his father, cursed to his dying day. Again, Simeon was held as hostage by Joseph in Egypt while his brothers went back to Canaan for Benjamin. The prison-house should have tamed him. It didn't.

He and his people settled near the Philistines. Given such neighbors, it was easy to fight. It was trouble and bloodshed from the start. At the census of Sinai Simeon had fifty-nine thousand three hundred fighting-men. At Moab, later, he had but twenty-two thousand two hundred. Wars wore them down. They grew weaker, less and less. Finally, for plain protection from the Canaanites, they joined with the tribe of Judah. Later, they merged with this tribe and disappeared.

They that take the sword shall perish with the sword.

*Genesis 29:33; 34:25 ff.; 42:24; 49:5 ff.;*
*Numbers 1:23; Numbers 26:14; Judges 1:3, 17.*

# *Levi*

WHEN LEAH'S THIRD SON ARRIVED, SHE THOUGHT:
"This time will my husband be joined unto me, for I
have borne him three sons." So she named him Levi,
meaning "joined." She still dared hope for some of the
affection bestowed on the placid Rachel. Disappointed
in that, she still had much in Levi to be thankful for.
The one black mark against him is that he wielded a
sword at Shechem.

But his descendants! What a host of memories is in
the very name, "Levites." They were the men set apart
for holy things. Priests. Teachers. Interpreters of the
Law. Guardians of the Ark. The Royal Guard of the
Unseen King. Vergers. Sacristans. Choristers. Chroni-
clers. They were to the people of Israel what ministers
and teachers are to us.

They held no lands, no territory. Cities for their use
and residence were assigned from the holdings of other
tribes. Six of these were "cities of refuge," to which un-
intentional criminals might flee. Levites, probably, sat
in the Sanhedrin which condemned Jesus.

Out of a family of thirteen, only one led a tribe of
priests. The usual proportion!

*Genesis 29:34; 34:25 ff.; Joshua 20:1-21:42.*

# Judah

THE ABLEST OF THE TWELVE BOYS, NEXT TO JOSEPH, was Judah. He was trustworthy, chivalrous, intelligent, silver-tongued, energetic.

It was Judah who persuaded his brothers to sell Joseph to the Ishmaelites rather than murder him.

It was Judah who was made responsible for the safety of young Benjamin on the hazardous second trip to Egypt.

It was Judah who delivered that golden oration before the governor of Egypt in the name of the aged father of both pleader and judge: "We have a father, an old man, and a child of his old age, a little one." Read it again. You will cry again—with the governor!

It was Judah who led old Jacob tenderly into the land of Goshen.

He had talent, and he used it. "A lion's whelp is Judah." He and his followers were richly blessed. This tribe was the strongest of them all; they always led the way. On their banners was the inscription, "Rise up, Lord, and let thine enemies be scattered." That, too, was the battle-cry of Cromwell's men at Dunbar.

Some interesting words have evolved from this man's name—"Judea," "Judas," "Jude," and "Jew."

*Genesis 29:35; 37:26 ff.; 43:3 ff.; 44:14 ff.;*
*46:28; 49:9; Numbers 10:35.*

# Dan

IN EVERY FAMILY OF BOYS, SOME ARE SURE TO MAKE great names for themselves, and some are sure to be forgotten, to leave almost no record at all behind them. Most of the sons of Jacob fall into the latter class. Dan was one of them.

Dan had but one son, yet his tribe was the second largest. When the promised land was cut up into twelve pieces, Dan's people got the smallest. They lost even that in a war with the Amorites. Driven into "the mountain," they lived out their days in leisure and repose.

Away up on the northern tip of the land is the city of Dan. It is the end, the jumping-off place. When people journeyed the length of the land, down to the southern tip, they spoke of going "from Dan to Beersheba." Today the city of Dan is a mere mound, and out of it bubbles one of the world's great fountains. It is the main source of the Jordan.

But wait! There was a famous strong man in Dan's tribe. He was a native of Zorah, Samson by name.

*Genesis 30:6; 46:23; Judges 13:2.*

# *Naphtali*

THE RECORDS OF THE LIFE OF NAPHTALI, SECOND SON of Bilhah, the slave, are also scant. The greatest events connected with his life happened at his birth, when he was a crying babe, or after his death, when the men of his tribe marched as a guard of honor beside the sacred tent on the long wilderness trek.

Rachel was childless when he was born, but she rejoiced over this son of her slave; she regarded this baby as a victory over Leah. "With great wrestlings have I wrestled with my sister," she cried, "and I have prevailed." Rachel named him Naphtali, which means, "wrestling."

At Sinai the tribe of Naphtali had fifty-three thousand four hundred fighting-men; at the entrance to the land of promise they had but forty-five thousand. They had lost heavily in wrestling with death, wilderness, and fatigue.

In the division of the kingdom, Naphtali belonged to Israel. Later they dwelt on the shores of blue Galilee, at Capernaum, and Bethsaida.

*Genesis 30:7; Deut. 33:23.*

# Gad

AND NOW ZILPAH, LEAH'S HANDMAID, HAS A SON. "Fortunate," she cried, and she named him Gad. There is a wealth of religious mythology behind that name. Gad was the title of an ancient Aramæan god of fortune. The Canaanites worshiped him; so did the Jews in Babylon.

Gad was Jacob's seventh, Zilpah's first-born son. The men of the tribe were fierce, warlike, and inclined to be a pastoral people. They settled finally, after the conquest of Canaan, in Gilead. Here they were overrun, in the times of the Judges, by the Ammonites. Jephthah delivered them. They supported the young David against Saul and they fought under the banners of Jeroboam. They went into captivity under Tiglath-Pileser when Ahaz was whipped by the union of Syria, Edom, and Israel.

The green slopes of Gilead! The land is more enchanting than its inhabitants. Here was Mahanaim, where Jacob met the angels, and Peniel, where he struggled. Ramoth-gilead, where Ahab was slain and where bloody Jehu was made Israel's king.

*Genesis 30:11; Numbers 32:34 ff.; Judges 11:4 ff.; II Chron. 28:16 ff.*

# *Asher*

ONE MORE CHILD WAS TO COME TO ZILPAH. HE WAS Asher. He was a hesitator who hesitated and was lost.

It was predicted that he should have many children, that he would "dip his foot in oil" (meaning that he should have rich olive groves), and that he was to be "shod with iron and brass" (from his mines in Lebanon). It all came true. But it all failed to do Asher much good.

His country boasted the richest soil in Palestine; it was on the seashore, stretching north from Carmel. Great crops leaped from the rich black earth, and fruit hung heavy on his trees. But, somehow, Asher and his tribe were indifferent, careless, lethargic. They put neither their talents nor their land to good account. They drifted slowly into unimportance.

It still happens. A good farmer may struggle to bring a pittance out of rocky soil, while a poor farmer, his very neighbor, will let crops rot in more fertile ground. Or a man with one talent never seems to get a chance, while a brilliant man goes down in dissipation.

Deborah, the prophetess, described him perfectly: "Asher sat still at the haven of the sea."

*Genesis 30:13; Deut. 33:24; Judges 5:17.*

# *Issachar*

LEAH'S FIFTH SON IS CONFUSING. HE HAS LEFT NOT ONE reputation, but two. On the one hand he has been called "a strong ass, couching down between two burdens," the inference being that Issachar was lazily content to dream among his flocks in Esdraelon, willing to submit to foreign domination rather than to fight back the invader. A "strong ass," able to work, he preferred to lie in the sun, regardless of the troubles of his brothers, or the march of time and men. But another translator says that Issachar only "desired the beautiful." That interpretation puts Issachar in an entirely different light. We excuse dreaming—in artists.

Either idea may be correct. Take your choice. It means little now—to Issachar.

His tribe gained no great renown. His country did. Across the Plain of Esdraelon have swarmed ages of conquerors. Egyptians, Canaanites, Philistines, have been there. Jews and Gentiles, Crusaders and Saracens, the Turk, the Frenchman and the Arab, have pitched camp on his plain.

History was made there, the fates of nations made and sealed. But not by Issachar.

*Genesis 30:18; 49:14; Joshua 19:17 ff.*

# *Zebulun*

THE RECORD OF ZEBULUN IS THE MOST MEAGER OF ALL. He is the "x," the unknown quantity, of the twelve. Like most of the northern tribes, he and his are the prisoners of obscurity.

The Book tells nothing of his character. There is no evidence whatever that his tribe either helped or hindered in the wilderness marching or in the conquest which followed. They blazed into action only once. That was against Sisera, when they stood shoulder to shoulder with the men of Naphtali. Deborah waxes eloquent about them here, saying that they ". . . jeoparded their lives unto the death upon the high places of the field." But they failed to vanquish the Canaanites, nevertheless. They should have had a rocket emblazoned on their banners, to symbolize their characters. Up like the rocket; down like the dead stick.

Odd that Zebulun should have been reared in the same home with Joseph, the most competent man in the Old Testament.

The hills of the Zebulun country shelter tiny Nazareth, where a Carpenter lived.

*Genesis 30:20; Judges 4:10; 5:18.*

# *Joseph*

YOU WERE THE NOBLEST MAN IN GENESIS, JOSEPH, the most fortunate and faultless. This was not a gift. It developed.

You were a spoiled boy once, the pet of your father, arrogant, dreamy, overbearing. Your haughtiness made your brothers furious. They sold you as a slave just to get rid of you.

You were better in Egypt, when you resisted the wiles of your master's wife and went to prison for it. Prison didn't break you; it gave you the strength of iron. You were comforter to your chained companions, interpreter of their dreams.

It was a lucky day when Pharaoh let you out of your cell to interpret *his* dream, a better day still when your interpretation proved true. How Pharaoh must have loved you to make you his Prime Minister! A lowly Hebrew slave boy, ruling Egypt!

What a noble you were when your brothers, driven by the whips of famine, stood before you. Your forgiveness was like Christ's. Your love passes understanding.

You were a brilliant, benevolent ruler. Success failed to spoil you. You prove to us that a good man, wherever he go, cannot put himself beyond God's care.

*Genesis 30:24; 37:2 ff.; 39-47.*

# Benjamin

BENJAMIN IS THE LAST OF THE SONS, THE LAST OF THE tribes. Rachel, with her dying breath, named him Benoni, "the son of my sorrow." But Jacob, crushed, could not bear that. The lad was renamed Benjamin, "son of the right hand."

The father lavished upon him the love he fain would have lavished upon Joseph. When he went off with his brothers to Egypt, the old man sobbed, ". . . if mischief befall him, then shall ye bring down my gray hairs with sorrow to the grave." Joseph loved the stalwart stripling, too, protected him, blessed him, wept over him, hid a silver cup in his baggage that he might see him again. No wonder. They were closer than brothers. Lovely-souled Rachel was mother to both.

Benjamin's tribesmen were unlike him. They were archers, skilled to deadly perfection in the use of the bow. There were great names among them: Saul the first king of Israel was a Benjamite; Paul of Tarsus, who boasted that he was "a Hebrew of the Hebrews," was another. Their territory lay north of Judah's. Men of war struggled there—Joshua, Sennacherib, Richard Coeur de Lion. The Man of Peace knew it too— Bethany, Jerusalem.

*Genesis 35:18; 42:38; 44:2 ff.; I Sam. 9:15 ff.;*
*10:24; Phil. 3:5.*

# *Shiphrah*

OVER SLUM DOORWAYS WE MAY STILL SEE THOSE little signs bearing the single word, "midwife." That word means much to those too poor to pay doctor or trained nurse; to the Israelites in Egypt it meant the preservation of their race.

Pharaoh, alarmed at the increasing Jewish population, resolved to wipe them out. Summoning the midwives of the slaves, he gave them a terrible command— "Kill every baby that is a boy." An early Massacre of the Innocents. To disobey meant death. Midwife Shiphrah and her sister midwives disobeyed. They saved their people from extinction. But for them Moses might have led a procession of women into Canaan. Without them, there might have been no Hebrews after Joseph.

Why do we pay such lazy tribute to our patriot women, such quick glory to our hero men? In the hearts of our Shiphrahs and Joans and Nightingales are fought first the really great battles of the world.

Shiphrah was more than a patriot. She saved Israel not for Israel's sake alone, but because "the midwives feared God." That is something higher than patriotism.

*Exodus 1:15.*

# *Jochebed*

FEAR CLUTCHED AT THE HEART OF JOCHEBED WHILE
Pharaoh's men were baby-hunting in the streets. Half in
panic and half in stratagem, she hid her baby boy in the
bulrushes by the river, near the pool where a princess
came down to bathe; left him, surely, with a prayer:
"Float, little boat. Guard him, God."

The princess found him, loved him when his baby
hands reached her cheek, took him home to the court of
her father. The baby cried. He needed a nurse, a Hebrew nurse. The baby's sister knew of one; she was sent
running to ask Jochebed to be "nurse" to her own
child!

"Give us your child until he is seven," says a great
church, "and I care not what you do with him afterward." Jochebed had her child through the plastic
years. Bit by bit, little by little, she poured into his ears
a love for his people and a reverence for their God.
Egypt could not hold him after that.

An uncommon mother in Israel. She disappears before the boy grows up. She never saw greatness come to
him.

"Give me your child until he is seven——"

*Exodus 2:1 ff.; 6:20.*

# *Thermouthis*

HER NAME IS NOT BIBLICAL; THERE SHE IS ONLY "THE daughter of Pharaoh." Tradition and the rabbis call her Thermouthis.

She was married and childless when she adopted Jochebed's baby. While Jochebed molded his heart, Thermouthis molded his mind. Jealously she planned for him, brought him up at a gorgeous court, had him trained in "all the wisdom of the Egyptians," saw him graduated from the university and ordained a priest in the Temple of On. She saw him rise to high military command. She made him heir to the throne of Egypt. She saw him with the world at his feet.

She laughed at him with her lips when he went "slumming" down among the miserable huts of the Hebrews; she wept for him in her heart when he killed a man and ran. It may be well she never knew he forsook the palaces of Egypt to lead a despised and degraded rabble of slaves into the desert.

Lest we forget, this Thermouthis gave the baby his name. She called him Moses, because she "drew him out of the water."

*Exodus 2:5 ff.; Acts 7:22.*

# *Moses*

MOSES IS MAGNIFICENT. GRANDEUR RESTS ON HIS mighty head like clouds on Sinai. In him humanity had a noble peak, God a great ambassador.

His youth he spent in Egypt, preparing. Oriental wise men taught him all they knew. He was their brilliant prodigy.

At forty he was a murderer, hiding in Midian. Royalty gave way to rags. He meditated, alone, in desert places. He brooded. A smoldering passion for his people in Egypt consumed him; a bush went ablaze before his eyes. God spoke: "Back to Egypt, Moses. Bring Israel out."

"Let my people go," he cries to Pharaoh as he leads them out. For forty years they follow him through the wilderness. He fights back enemy raiders, puts down dissension in his ranks. He gives Jewry unity and law, morality, faith, God, worship. He is deliverer, conqueror, lawgiver, prophet. He makes a nation out of a mob.

He served not only Israel, but left his mark on the social structure, thinking, ethics, and religion of all humanity. No man ever had more to contend with and no man, alone, has helped his brothers more.

Death took him, dramatically, at the very gates of Canaan.

*Exodus 2:11 ff.; 5:1; Deut. 34:5.*

# *Miriam*

LEADER OF EXODUS WOMEN WAS MIRIAM, SISTER OF Moses. Her life is a drama in four acts.

Act One: As a mere child she saved the life of her baby brother. Quick-witted, she restored Moses to Jochebed.

Act Two: She beats a tambourine, dancing for joy as Pharaoh's army drowns in the sea. She leads a wild "Te Deum":

"Sing ye to Jehovah, for he hath triumphed gloriously:
The horse and his rider hath he thrown into the sea."

She is a prophetess in this Act, like the prophets of Samuel and Saul, expressing herself in poetry, music, and parade.

Act Three: She is disgraced. She has rebelled against Moses, muttering enviously: "Hath the Lord indeed spoken only by Moses? Hath he not spoken also by us?" For this religious impertinence she is afflicted with leprosy—and cured at the prayer of Moses!

Act Four: She is restored to favor, and in favor she dies at Kadesh, where "there was no water for the congregation." She is the first of the sacred family of the three deliverers to die. She is still honored, as prophetess and patriot, by the Jews.

*Exodus 2:4; 15:20; Numbers 12:1 ff.; 20:1.*

# *Aaron*

THE MAGIC WAND OF GREATNESS NEVER TOUCHED THE shoulder of Aaron. Older than Moses in years, he was younger in genius and character.

In Egypt he was his brother's mouthpiece, the bumper between the elders and the people, between Pharaoh and Israel as well. He did the talking.

He also did the praying. He was the senior member of that distinguished clan of high-priests of Levi which held sway over Israel for sixteen hundred years. He was the instrument of most of the Exodus miracles. He loved God.

He was eloquent but unstable; witness his erection of the golden calf and his ridiculous explanation: He was weak in danger and irresolute; witness his willingness to let Miriam take the whole blame for their foolhardy little rebellion. He was strong so long as he had Moses to lean upon. But when left to himself he was quite apt to fail. Such men are valuable, but we cannot trust them far.

His life is a study in chaos. Promise and uncertainty fought for him. Uncertainty won. He died in disgrace, stripped of his priestly robe and office.

The mind of Moses dominated him and left him weak.

*Exodus 4:15, 30; 17:12 ff.; 32:21;*
*Numbers 12:10; 20:25 ff.*

# *Hur*

AARON LEANED HEAVILY ON MOSES. MOSES LEANED heavily on Hur, who was a subordinate captain of the host. That's a habit great men have. Their halos are handed up to them by their subalterns. Without their subalterns—what? Where might our "great industrial princes" be without the men in their shops? Or Pershing without his doughboys?

Israel fought Amalek at Rephidim, under General Joshua. Moses prayed for victory. So long as his hands were lifted toward heaven, Israel prevailed. When they drooped, Israel had the worst of it. The arms grew tired, weary, "heavy," and when Moses could hold them high no longer, Hur came, with Aaron, and held them up, "until the going down of the sun." Israel won.

Later, with Aaron again, he was left in charge of the people while Moses ascended Sinai. Some claim he married Miriam.

We are not all of Moses' caliber, but we may all steady our leaders' hands. That is, if we are willing to sacrifice a halo for a "Well done, good and faithful servant." Being a good supporter is often harder than being a good leader.

*Exodus 17:12; 24:14.*

# Joshua

BEHOLD AN OFFICER AND A GENTLEMAN, ONE OF THE precious few of us whose memory bears no stain. Egypt gave him birth. Fighting in Canaan made him the patrician of soldiery. Moses, dying, named him his successor. A good choice.

Joshua was one of the twelve spies to go first into Canaan, one of two to tell the truth of what he saw. At Rephidim he won his spurs, giving blow for blow with Amalek while Moses prayed on a hill. He earned his epaulets at Jericho, where he drove a wedge of spears deep into the enemy-land. Gibeon and Ai but clinched his fame.

He never was more than a dutiful soldier, an under-officer of Jehovah. When the wars were done we hear little more of him, except that he divided the land and preached two good sermons. Read them if you are sermon-weary. They sparkle.

He gained a country, united a people to hold it. He was fearless in battle, sharp as a fox in strategy, a wise councilor and a whole-hearted servant of his people and his God. A Babe born in a manger was given his name: "Jesus" is Greek for "Joshua."

*Exodus 17:8 ff.; Numbers 13:8; 14:6; Deut. 1:37; Joshua 5:13 ff.; 8:1 ff.; 9:3 ff.; 23:24.*

# *Eldad*

THE SPIRIT OF THE LORD DESCENDED, ONE FINE DAY, to rest upon seventy elders. The seventy immediately became prophets. (Not predictors, but ecstatic exhorters.) Moses gathered them together in the tabernacle for a prayer-meeting. Two of them wouldn't come.

Eldad and Medad "got the Spirit," while among the people of the camp, and among the people, they insisted, they would stay to prophesy. Joshua objected to that: "My lord Moses, forbid them." Moses refused. The Spirit of the Lord, he felt, was the property of no selected person, place, or class; it is no respecter of persons; it belongs to all. Open prayer-meetings in the camp might be as effective as "closed" prayer-meetings in the tent. We can almost hear Moses sigh as he says, wistfully, "Would that all the Lord's people were prophets, that the Lord would put his Spirit upon them."

Millions in America still confine religion to a church building.

*Numbers 11:24 ff.*

# Caleb

OF THE DOZEN SENT TO SPY OUT CANAAN, TEN WERE poltroons and two were men. Only Joshua and Caleb said, "Go in and take it." Would Joshua, alone, one against eleven, have dared to say that? Caleb gave courage to Joshua, weight to the truth.

A proselyte of Judah's tribe, he gained no epaulets, no laurel wreaths. He was content to serve well and live quietly. Yet he did better than most of us can do—"He wholly followed the Lord." He was rewarded, with Joshua, by being spared to enter the Land of Promise.

Forty-five years later he appears again, asking Joshua for a land-grant in the hills of Hebron. He got it—and with it a war. The "sons of Anak" vexed him so sorely that he offered his daughter in marriage to the man who could drive them out. His brother Othniel got the girl.

A child of the future, looking always into Canaan and never into Egypt, Caleb was forty years ahead of his times. That's why he was in the minority group.

The seers of history have been hated by their own generation, loved and lauded by the next.

*Numbers 13:30; 14:6 ff.; 24; 32:12; Joshua 14:6 ff.; Judges 1:12 ff.*

# Achsah

MEN RULED IN THE HEBREW HOME, AND WOMEN FOUND it convenient to obey. Jehovah's command to Eve was their domestic law, "He [thy husband] shall rule over thee." Rarely did they dare assert themselves. Rarely, we meet within their ranks a lively little rebel such as Achsah, that daughter of Caleb who was offered as a prize of war and won by Othniel. Achsah was a prize—in more ways than one.

Caleb, at her marriage, gave her for a dowry a piece of land in waterless Negeb. Achsah looked at it, decided it was not good enough, rode over to her father's home and demanded "springs of water" to make it fertile. Some Oriental fathers would have been speechless at such feminine presumption. But Achsah knew her father. She got the springs.

Dull historians say it is just a story to account for the springs' coming into the possession of the Othnielites of Debir when they really belonged to the Calebites of Hebron. But those with a little romance left in their blood see in the little rebel a courage and an independence and a spirit of adventure which make her far more attractive than a drab, submissive menial.

*Joshua 15:16 ff.*

# *Korah*

CALEB HELPED. KORAH OBSTRUCTED. HE OPENED A Pandora's box of jealousies and fears which nearly brought disaster.

Korah had a grievance. He and his men wanted high office and they couldn't get it. They were being excluded from the high-priesthood. Plotting to get it, they whipped up the already ugly whispers of dissatisfaction among the wanderers, stood brazenly at last before Moses in open rebellion. It all ended as dramatically as it had begun: an earthquake, a fire, and a plague brought about their destruction. ". . . and they perished from among the congregation."

Korah had a grievance. He and his men wanted high office to be on constant guard; in those who rebelled with him the fickleness and cowardice of the Exodus men are at their worst. "Is it a small thing that thou hast brought us up out of a land flowing with milk and honey, to kill us in the wilderness?" Exactly! Men inevitably turn on their saviors. They want honey, not salvation.

Korah was a dissenter. Now a good dissenter is a delight. But a mercenary office-seeker—no.

*Numbers 16:1 ff.*

# *Balak*

King Balak of Moab, like his neighbor King Arad, looked down from his mountains and saw the tents of the Israelites spread like grasshoppers over his land. Balak feared them, too, and he set about the business of crushing them. First he made an alliance with the Midianites. E Pluribus Unum. Then he sent for a famous Chaldean sage and prophet and soothsayer to put a curse on the enemy.

This soothsayer, Balaam, was a great disappointment to Balak. Instead of cursing, he blessed. Balak offered him money, treasure without end, to anathematize. But Balaam just couldn't do it. God wouldn't let him, he said. Even if Balak were to offer him "his house full of silver and gold," he couldn't do it. And that was that.

Alas, poor Balak. You thought money could buy anything, even to the favor of God. Did you know in your heart that God is not mocked, nor bought? You were a frustrated Canute, trying to hold back an inevitable, relentless wave with a bribed prophet. Suppose you *had* won Balaam, would you have believed the curse, yourself?

Enlightening, is it not, that Balak sought God's help?

*Numbers 22:2 ff.*

# *Balaam*

BALAAM WAS A WELL WITHOUT WATER, A CLOUD CAR-
ried with a tempest. He had the gift but lacked the grace
of a great prophet. He could foretell by magic, but he
could not exemplify by self-denial. He reached for
heaven, almost touched it—then dropped back.

Conflicting voices tore his soul and left the Spirit flut-
tering there like a spent candle. He loved money; Balak's offer staggered him, yet he refused it. He loved
God, yet was never sure of Him. He stood first on one
foot, then on the other, seeking balance. His soul died
when he suggested sensual corruption as a weapon
against Israel. His body perished as he fought with
Midian—against Israel.

Yet he had much merit. Three times Balak tempted
him, three times he fought it down. His courage was su-
perb. It was not easy to bless Israel in Balak's camp,
with treasure and high position calling. He let God
speak through him, and that was hard.

If his sense of holiness had been as keen as his sense
of necromancy, we should link his name with the great
Isaiah's.

*Numbers 22:5-24:25; 31:7, 16.*

# Rahab

TWO SPIES SNEAKED INTO JERICHO TO SKETCH THE fortifications and list the strength of Jericho's regiments. They were discovered, and ran for shelter to an inn on the city wall, owned by one Rahab, a harlot. (Josephus says she was no more than an innkeeper.) When the king's soldiers came, Rahab buried the spies under stalks of flax on her roof. "They went that way," she said to the pursuers, pointing down the road. While they were off on their fool's errand, she dropped a scarlet cord out of her window and over the wall, and the spies slid down to safety.

When the men of Joshua took the city, they spared Rahab and her family. Hanging in her window was a signal—a piece of scarlet cord.

Were you really scarlet, you Rahab of the scarlet cord? If you were, you repented and changed, for you were the mother of Boaz and the ancestress of Jesus. If you were, you were surely pardoned, for you had both faith *and* works.

If you were scarlet in the eyes of men, you were gold in the sight of God, you and all your sisters in the sorority of shame.

*Joshua 2:1 ff.*

# *Achan*

THE JEWS BURNED JERICHO, THEN LOOTED IT. NOW
loot was the property of all, thrown in a common chest
for the common weal. But Achan, of the tribe of Judah,
did a bit of looting for himself. He stole a "Babylonish
garment, and two hundred shekels of silver and a wedge
of gold," and buried them in the dirt floor of his tent.
That was unfortunate, as unfortunate as the albatross
hung on the neck of the Ancient Mariner. Disaster visited
Israel when Ai was stormed; thirty-six were left dead on
the field. Alarmed, Joshua searched and found the "ac-
cursed thing" in Achan's tent. Achan was stoned and
burned and buried in a criminal's grave, beneath a heap
of stones.

Thirty-six died for his covetousness. More than this
suffered when he died. That's the worst of coveting. It
maims not only the coveter, but takes wide toll of the
innocent. Sin is never a "personal" affair; its effects and
implications are social.

You were a fool, Achan. What did you want with a
Babylonish garment and a handful of silver? What does
any thief or coveter want——?

*Joshua 7:1 ff.*

# Ehud

Othniel was the first of the great judges; he delivered the Hebrew from the Mesopotamian. Ehud was the second; he conquered Moab.

Ehud was left-handed and strong. He went one day to deliver a "present" to King Eglon, the Moabite warrior who had recaptured Jericho to hold it eighteen years. Conniving a secret interview in the "summer parlor" of the king, Ehud presented his gift, jerked a two-edged dagger from his belt, and with his powerful left hand drove it deep into the body of the king. "And Eglon," says the writer, "was a very fat man . . . and the fat closed upon the blade, so that he could not draw the dagger out." The killer slipped away, after locking the door, climbed the steep cliffs or quarries behind Jericho, gathered his men, seized the fords of the Jordan through which the Moabites must pass in pursuit or flight, and cut them off. They killed ten thousand Moabites.

It may all pass for patriotism, but it sounds suspiciously like cold-blooded murder. It was the order of the day.

*Judges 3:12 ff.*

# Barak

King Jabin of Canaan came like a hailstorm out of the north, driving nine hundred war chariots of iron with sharp knives at their wheels, spreading terror and death as a pall. Captain of the iron chariots was Sisera, mighty man of battles.

Captain Barak, with his little army on Mt. Tabor, watched them come. "Barak" means "lightning-flash." He struck like that. He came down from Tabor to face the metal-shod horror, marched to Megiddo to attack. As the battle began a driving storm broke from the east, terrifying the horses of Sisera, stampeding the army of Jabin into the swollen, angry torrent of the "river Kishon." The rest was easy for Barak.

"The stars in their courses fought against Sisera. The river of Kishon swept them away. . . ." Those who fight nobly for a noble cause have God ("the stars") on their side.

Give not all the credit to Barak. A woman inspired him.

Another woman found Sisera in her tent, cringing, unnerved after the rout. She was Jael, wife of Heber.

*Judges 4 and 5.*

# *Jael*

~~~~~~~~~~~~~~~~~~~~~~~~~~~~~~~~~~~~~~~~~~

"FEAR NOT," SHE SAID TO THE FUGITIVE SISERA, AS SHE covered him, on the floor of her tent, with a rug. She stood guard for him at the tent flap, sending searchers away. When he asked for water to drink, she brought him milk. When at last he dropped off to sleep from sheer exhaustion, she covered his head with her rug, took up a hammer and a long tent-pin, and neatly drove the long spike through his brain. Captain Barak found him there, nailed to the floor.

One of the most dramatic lines in Scripture pictured the old mother of Sisera waiting for him to come home, looking out of her window:

> "The mother of Sisera cried through the lattice,
>   Why is his chariot so long in coming?"

What do *you* make of Jael? Assassin or righteous avenger? Patriot or fiend? Charlotte Corday or Joan of Arc?

Deborah said she was "blessed above all women"! This was the same Deborah who had inspired Barak.

*Judges 4:17 ff.; 5:24.*

62

# *Deborah*

═══════════════════════════════════

IT IS RIDICULOUS, BUT IT IS TRUE: AT THAT HOUR IN
Israel's history when Israel needed most the mind of a
Moses and the arm of a Joshua, Israel was led by a
woman. By Deborah, who was an Achsah magnified.
She was a rebel who dominated.

At first she was no more than a homemaker and a
"mother in Israel." Then she was a judge, sitting under
a palm tree and holding informal court on her peers.
Then she was counselor to all.

She saw the oppression of the Canaanites and the
idolatry of Israel. Her blood boiled. She became a
human torch, stirring the men to fighting fury, the
women to sacrifice. She became military dictator,
directing the battle against King Jabin and winning it.

Then she became poetess, breaking into song. The
"Song of Deborah" has few equals in literature.

She lived in a wild and barbarous hour, and she was
a creature of her hour. She exhorted and commanded
thousands in war as prophetess, statesman, judge.

What would she be doing were she alive today?

*Judges 4:4-5:31.*

# Gideon

A BOY WHO TORE DOWN ALTARS WAS GIDEON, "LEAST
in [his] father's house," but destined to be a national
hero, prophet, warrior, and judge.

He won always by surprise. He won his greatest battle with an army of three hundred [picked from out ten
thousand] armed each with a trumpet, a lamp, and an
earthenware jar.

He fought long and gloriously for Israel. He knew
God's voice when he heard it. But he falls short of the
heroism model of Moses and Joshua. He was cautious.
His faith depended on facts and figures. Question marks
occur as often in his record as exclamation marks. He
refused to be a king: "Only God is your King," he says
to Israel. Exclamation mark! But he made an ephod of
the golden spoil of Midian. Question mark!

Yet by prestige of his sword—and intermarriage—he
built up a kingdom in the heart of Israel. It was the nation's first attempt at kingdomizing. It collapsed.

*Judges 6:11-8:32.*

# *Baal*

BAAL IS OLDER THAN THE BIBLE. ANCIENT PHOENICIA, Babylon, Greece, and Egypt worshiped him. Him? Baal is not one, but a galaxy of gods.

When Israel changed in Canaan from a race of rovers to a race of farmers, they met with the belief that every spot of fertile ground owed its fertility to the presence of some supernatural power, or Baal. Wherever there was a green tree or a cool, bubbling spring, some Baal lived. And inasmuch as they were now dependent for their very lives upon the soil, they soon began to seek the favor of these gods of fertility. In their worship, more than in the gods, lay the deep-seated evil which the prophets and Gideon feared and fought; it was a low nature-worship, disgustingly sensuous, an excuse for indecency and a peril to character and faith. A religion which "excuses" is always attractive—and always fatal. It is the religion which stands for nobility in life and personality which is always hard—and always valuable.

Judged against their agricultural background, the bowing of Israel to Baal is not hard to understand. Christian farmers still pray for rain (*without* licentiousness).

*Judges 2:13; 3:7; 6:25 ff.; Jeremiah 7:8 ff.*

# *Ashtoreth*

A NOTED ANIMAL-HUNTER HAS SAID THAT AMONG THE beasts the tiger is one without a single redeeming feature in his makeup. Ashtoreth is the tigress of deities.

To the Phœnicians and the Canaanites she was the female companion of Baal; she was called Ishtar by the Assyrians and Astarte by the Greeks. Some hold that Baal was god of the sun, Ashtoreth goddess of the moon; some that Baal was Jupiter, and Ashtoreth Venus or Aphrodite. One name is as good as another. Whatever, whoever she was, she was far worse than Baal.

She is the goddess of untrammeled sexual love, goddess of maternity and fertility, of war, decay, and death. In her temples were armies of young prostitutes, condemned for life to act in her bawdry rituals. At her shrine bestiality was king, sex license unconfined.

There may be some excuse for a primitive farmer worshiping Baal; there seems little for a monarch like Solomon bowing to Ashtoreth.

Let it be said here to the credit of Israel that she finally deserted Ashtoreth for Jehovah; that she fought down the lewdness of Venus-worship and produced a God in Christ.

*Judges 2:13; 10:6; 1 Kings 11:5.*

# *Abimelech*

OF ALL THE ROGUES OF HOLY WRIT, ABIMELECH IS king. King by unholy right of murder.

Son of Gideon by a Shechemite concubine, he used his mother's people to overcome his father's. With the help of Shechem and a gang of hired cut-throats he reared a throne and sat upon it. He brooked no competition, no pretenders. In one night, on a single stone, he cut the throats of all his seventy brothers save one. Jotham got away.

At that, his throne soon shook him off. Shechem rebelled, twice. Once Abimelech, riding like Sheridan at Winchester, put them down. At the second a woman of Thebez leaned from a tower window, dropped a millstone on his head, and cracked his skull. Brute-hearted to the end, he called his armor-bearer: "Draw thy sword, and slay me, that men say not of me, a woman slew him. And his young man thrust him through. . . ."

An unprincipled adventurer, ruthlessly ambitious, snarling, sinister. "Might makes right" was his creed. He had courage; he knew how and when to seize authority and how to hold it. But his masculinity was powerless against the suicidal poison of that creed.

*Judges 8:31; 9:5; 9:22 ff.*

# Jotham, Son of Jerubbaal

JOTHAM HID HIMSELF AND ESCAPED ABIMELECH'S massacre. Then he hid again. When he heard of the crowning of Abimelech, he came out of hiding, preached a fiery sermon on a mount, and ran to hide again.

In the sermon is a parable, of vines and brambles and fig trees. (A sermon-method Jesus used.) In it the preacher takes the men of Shechem to task for selecting such a one as king when finer men were waiting. Shechem was quite like some cities of our own—charlatans steered the ship of state while better men stayed clear.

In the sermon also is a prayer, biting, sarcastic, blunt (a prayer-method Jesus never used). When prayer and parable failed to work, Jotham invoked a curse. The curse worked. Both Shechem and Shechem's king settled their accounts in the coin of violence.

If you look sharp, you may find a note of frustrated ambition in that sermon. Jotham felt himself to be the legitimate heir of Gideon's sword and rule. But like Oliver Cromwell's son, he was hardly big enough. . . .

Rear a throne, anywhere, and find a host of quarreling heirs at your palace door!

*Judges 9:5 ff.*

# *Gaal*

GAAL FLASHES IN AND OUT, LIKE HALLEY'S COMET. HE appeared from nowhere, talking of how fine things would be if *he* were king. Soon it was a case of Gaal *vs.* Abimelech, adventurer *vs.* adventurer, diamond cut diamond.

Like Abimelech before him, he played up the race question, got the men of Shechem in a fighting fury under an old, moth-eaten slogan, "Shechem for the Shechemites." Foolishly, he defied Abimelech to "Increase thine army, and come out." Abimelech came out, fighting. Gaal was trapped, routed, crushed. His city was smashed and the very ground on which it stood was sowed with salt.

Gaal cuts a poor figure. He was little, lacking everything a real soldier ought to have. He should be a horrible example; too many of his kind have duped nations into needless war. "Shechem for the Shechemites" is always a handy slogan for the devil's architects. "Patriotism" may be either a laudable virtue or it may be a tool in the hands of a scheming loon.

# Jephthah

HE NEVER SMILED. TRAGEDY ENVELOPED HIM LIKE A great black cloak. Born out of wedlock, he was driven from his Gilead home by his "legitimate" brothers, to become the bold and successful captain of a band of freebooters in the land of Tob. When Ammon bested his brothers in war, they came begging the bandit brother to deliver them. He saved them and ruled them till he died.

Anxious for victory against Ammon, Jephthah made the rash bargain and vow with Jehovah for which he is immortal. If he won, then "whatsoever cometh forth from the doors of my house to meet me . . . I will offer it up for a burnt offering." His own suspecting, lovely daughter came to meet him. Jephthah kept his vow. Thereafter, he "lived alone in a world of moan."

He is a good example of the Judges deliverer. Narrow in faith, but intense; brave, but rash and short-sighted; cruel, but regarding himself as the agent of Deity. That was Jephthah.

Loyal. Loving. Tragically beautiful. Sad that she had but one life to give for her people—that was Jephthah's daughter. Was God pleased as she was sacrificed? Which was greater? Father? Daughter?

*Judges 11:1 ff.*

# *Samson*

SAMSON IS THE BIBLE'S HERCULES. HE KILLED A LION with his bare hands; slaughtered a thousand Philistines with the jawbone of an ass; caught three hundred foxes, tied their tails together, set them loose in the Philistines' corn. His stealing of the great city gates of Gaza was the prank of an overgrown boy let loose on Hallowe'en.

Fighting was his forte. Like the baby Hannibal, he had been dedicated to it. The trouble was that it was all muscle-fighting. He never used his brain. He had a giant body and a pygmy mind. Unconquerable physically, he was worse than a baby in the hands of a pretty woman. Unlike Abimelech, a woman conquered him!

Still, he had his points. He stood and fought when even mighty Judah's tribe ran from the field. He worshiped God, while they deserted to idols. In the midst of a nation disrupted he was a militant, solitary, defiant soul.

His feuds were personal, his story an accumulation of village tales. Read it with one eye open to pity, the other to Samson's background.

*Judges 13:24; 14:1; 16:31.*

# *Delilah*

TAKE THE TEN LOWEST WOMEN FROM EVE TILL NOW, multiply by ten and find Delilah, Philistine courtesan. She and honor never met. In her face was the beauty which lured Samson; in her heart, dark as a pool at midnight, was the viperous treachery which led him to blindness, bonds, and death.

She never loved him. She sold him to his enemies as readily as she would have sold a cat. Mercilessly as a spider weaving his web, she set her net for Samson; she coaxed, she wept, she used every fatal feminine charm until at last she knew. With his head in her lap, asleep, she held him as the Philistine barber cut his hair. And he, poor beauty-smitten, dreaming fool, "wist not that the Lord was departed from him."

Not so much in his hair as in his consecration to God (of which the uncut hair was symbol) lay Samson's strength—lies any man's strength. When that bond is cut we are weaker than children.

Milton, in *Samson Agonistes,* tries hard to redeem her, but even sonorous Milton pleads a hopeless case. Delilah is queen of obloquy; no father has ever given his child her name.

*Judges 16:4 ff.*

# Naomi

MARVEL AT THE BOOK OF RUTH. WEDGED IN BETWEEN the bloody struggles of the Judges and the Kings, it is an oasis of loveliness, as arresting as a strain of Beethoven in a "Y" hut on the Marne.

It tells of Naomi, who married and went to Moab. There death took her husband and her sons, leaving her only poverty, grief, and two widowed daughters-in-law. Stout-hearted, she started back to her own people. "You stay with yours," she bids the widows, Ruth and Orpah. They would find no husbands among the foreigners in Naomi's Bethlehem; in Moab they would rewed.

One, weeping, stayed in Moab. The other went with crushed Naomi, to glean in the fields of a rich kinsman. Now the mother-in-law becomes matchmaker; she manages the marriage of Ruth and Boaz. One day she clutched Ruth's baby to her heart. The baby was Obed, grandsire to King David.

Hard critics call Naomi a schemer, self-pitying, self-seeking, egotistical. They forget that she wanted to go alone to Bethlehem. She schemed against Boaz? Well— what of that? Must we hate a hen scratching for her chicks?

*Ruth 1:1 ff.; 3:1 ff.; 4:17.*

# *Orpah*

ORPAH TOOK NAOMI AT HER WORD. SHE WEPT, SHE kissed the Spartan mother-in-law and clung to her when bidden to go back to her "own house," but back she went. She preferred husbands in Moab to exile with Naomi and Ruth.

Hear her whole story before you pass sentence. Marriage was the great dream, then as now, in every maiden's heart. To be the mother, especially the mother of a son, was and is the highest honor open to the Eastern woman. Orpah wanted—that. And she saw little chance of getting it in Naomi's land, where Moabites, male or female, were genuinely hated.

Her name means "gazelle," or "freshness of youth." She was young. Life's door had just been flung open in her face. And life would not be life at all, except in Moab.

It was a choice of loves she had, a conflict of loyalties. It may be that Orpah chose unwisely, for she drops out of sight, while the name of Ruth still lives.

*Ruth 1:6 ff.*
74

# *Ruth*

~~~~~~~~~~~~~~~~~~~~~~~~~~~~~~~~~~~~~~~~~~~~~~~~~~

WAS WORDSWORTH THINKING OF HER AS HE WROTE—

"She was a Phantom of delight . . ."?

Ruth was better even than this. She transcended phantomness, to be indeed "a perfect woman, nobly planned." She was Delilah's opposite; attractiveness of face and sex were glorified, outdone by the pure love and unselfish pity of her soul.

In self-forgetting loyalty to her dead husband's family, she chose to go with Naomi: "Entreat me not to leave thee . . . for whither thou goest, I will go; . . . thy people shall be my people, and thy God my God." For Naomi's sake she faced race prejudice and (which is worse?) religious animosity. She sweetly overcame them both, and in the end married a Hebrew!

Ruth gleaning food for old Naomi: there she is priceless. Ruth commanding the respect of all who saw her by her very bearing and gentleness; Ruth the "foreigner," loved for her own golden spirit in spite of clashing gods and national boundary lines: there she is sublime.

Her age is gone, her sickle is rust. But Dr. Fosdick poignantly wonders: "We have improved on Ruth's sickle as an agricultural implement, but have we improved on Ruth?"

*Ruth 1:15 ff.; 2:1 ff.; 4:7 ff.*

# *Boaz*

IF ALL MEN WERE LIKE BOAZ, THE KINGDOM OF GOD would come with tomorrow. He was a man wealthy, jovial, manly, hard-working. He had no use for little creeds; the little manmade tags of blood and ritual were not for him.

He married Ruth the Moabitess, thereby cutting clean across the thinking of his age and stepping out ahead of it. Here is the bold marriage of the Gentile and the Jew, the prophecy, in fact, of a day when, under a descendant of Boaz, many would "come from the east and the west . . . and sit down with Abraham and Isaac and Jacob in the Kingdom of God." Dr. Matheson puts it: "In the soul of Jesus the wedding-bells of Ruth and Boaz ring once more."

They miss the point who think of this book as only a pastoral idyl. It is a pertinent gospel for the treatment of "foreigners."

It is good to pray at Christmas for "peace on earth, goodwill to men," but to get that, men, in breadth of mind and depth of heart, must be more like Boaz than they are.

*Ruth 2:1 ff.; 4:1 ff.; Matthew 8:11.*

# Hannah

ON HER KNEES IN THE TEMPLE AT SHILOH SHE BEGGED God for a child. A man-child, to be given to the service of the Lord. She prayed so ardently that the high priest thought her drunk. But when he knew, he blessed her.

Hannah persevered in prayer, and Samuel was born. She broke into song then, into a wild, exultant shout of victory. It is prophetic poetry at its best, this song of Hannah's; it is the Old Testament Magnificat on which the Virgin Mary built her song when Jesus came.

She left him in the temple, in charge of patriarchal Eli, to learn to serve the Lord. She missed him. At home she spent long hours making little coats for him, holy vestments stitched in love, fit for a temple-child. But she never asked him to come home. She had given her word. Unlike Samson, this child was successfully consecrated; he was the true son of his mother's vows.

Womanly, candid, graceful, she typifies the ultimate in mother-love, in spiritual joy and renunciation. Persistent, praying prayers fragrant with simple faith: such was Hannah, mother of Samuel.

*I Samuel 1:9-2:21.*

# *Eli*

ELI IS OLD WHEN WE SEE HIM FIRST, SITTING (ALWAYS sitting) "by a post of the temple of the Lord." Life flowed past his door and he hardly knew it.

He ruled at Shiloh in that day between the passing of the Judges and the coming of the Kings. The turmoil of the changing day bewildered him. He knew not what to do. His own sons (priests, following him) profaned the priesthood and defiled the Ark; Eli was timid and weak in his rebuke. For that his house was destroyed and the Ark lost.

Eli loved that Ark. The rules of its worship were to him the rules of life. When he learned (*"sitting* by the wayside!"*) that the Philistines had captured it, he fell from his seat and died.

No one doubts his piety or consecration. Everyone regrets that while he loved the Ark and temple of the Lord, he never built arks or temples in human hearts, nor more stately mansions in the soul.

Or did he build something like that in those long years while he was training Samuel?

*I Samuel 1:9; 2:12 ff.; 4:12 ff.*

# Samuel

"SAMUEL, SAMUEL," CALLED THE LORD. ISRAEL'S MAN of the Hour, her Man of Destiny, was being summoned. In some ways he is greater than Moses. The Deliverer created a nation and a faith. Samuel restored them, re-created them when they lay in ruins.

With Hannah's nature and Eli's tutelage, "Samuel grew, and Jehovah was with him." Eli died, and the reins were his. He was everywhere, praying, exhorting, calling his people back to the faith of their fathers, re-kindling the flame of high religious life. New zeal and strength possessed them; they fell on the Philistines and crushed them. The religio-political reformation was complete when Samuel made Saul a king. The first king! Judgeship passes; kingship and monarch have come.

King or no king, Samuel still remained the power behind the throne. As the first religious educationist he inaugurated a "School of Prophets," headed, himself, that line of prophets who were to personify the national conscience, keep the kings in line and the people true to Jehovah.

King-maker, rebuilder, governmental centralizer, national unifier, dispeller of decadence—Samuel! There walked a man.

*I Samuel 3:10 ff.; 7:3 ff.; 10:17 ff.; 19:19 ff.*

# *Saul*

YOUNG SAUL WAS IMPRESSIVE, STANDING HEAD AND shoulders above his countrymen. Tall. Handsome. Strong. Modest. Every inch a king. At mere sight of him the assembled nation cheered; for the first time in Israel a shout rang out: "God save the king." God tried to. Saul interfered.

He started well. One after another he fought down his enemies. Philistines, Ammonites, Moabites, Amalekites, and Syrians he overcame. Then, at the height of his popularity and power, he tried to reckon without his God, and his house came down on his head.

Drunk with sight of power, he ignored God's voice and sought that of a witch at Endor. The fine mind crumbled, fits of madness, jealousy, and melancholy made him a periodic lunatic. To end it all he leaped on his own sword. The Philistines struck off his head and hung his body on their city wall.

In his better moments Saul was likable and royal. But for that taint of insanity and that streak of jealousy and rash arrogance, he might have been a leader on Israel's roll of kings. All in all, as kings go, he was good enough.

A boy with a slingshot and a pebble got his kingdom.

*1 Samuel 10:23 ff.; 11:1-16:23 ff.; 31:4 ff.*

# Witch of Endor

ONCE HE HAD HATED HER, TRIED TO DRIVE HER, WITH the rest of "those that had familiar spirits . . . out of the land." Now, with Samuel dead, his life and kingdom breaking up, the once-strong king creeps across the mountains in disguise, under midnight stars, to sit before her witch's fire. It is the last resort. "Bring me up Samuel," he piteously pleads.

Then she knew him ". . . thou art Saul!" She trembled, and in trembling called her ghost of Samuel and hovered in the shadows while king and specter talked. She heard the ghost tell the monarch that death would call for him at dawn. She saw the ghost depart, the king fall fainting on her earthen floor.

For days she cared for him. She offered him bread, which he refused; then a fatted calf, killed in his honor, which he ate.

A witch? Surely she was no two-toothed hag, like the harpies of "Macbeth." Her gentleness with the distracted king, her soothing words, her loaf of witch's bread and fatted calf, lift her above them. There was a bit of the angel in Endor's witch.

*1 Samuel 28:3 ff.*

# *Goliath*

BEHEMOTH GOLIATH STOOD ON A HILL AND FILLED THE land with his roaring. Ten feet six in his armor he stood, the tip of his spear weighing twenty pounds, his breastplate one hundred and fifty. Every day for forty days he bellowed at Saul's army. "Send out a man to fight me." No man came. David came, walking into fame and history.

With the rival armies looking on, he faced the monster. A good little man against a good big one. The giant sneered and roared and drew his spear; the stripling spun a pebble in his shepherd's sling, smashed it neatly between Goliath's eyes, hacked off his head while he lay stunned. Israel, suddenly brave, ran for the Philistines.

It is an old story, older than the hills they fought upon. And an old custom, this settling of national disputes by individual combat, found in every people's literature of heroism. Yet, young David has stunned the ages with his pebble. Great genius plus great faith plus a slingshot in the hands of a shepherd boy and a minstrel to King Saul: men will daydream over that so long as there are men.

*1 Samuel 17:4 ff.*

# *David*

MOST MEN DO ONE THING WELL AND CALL IT ENOUGH. David did many things well and died in grief. He is Many-sided David, the personification of his nation's many-sided development, "the embodiment of her qualities, the incarnation of her spirit, the type of her destiny."

He was a saint. Pure religion lay within him like hidden gold; applied religion was at its best in his perennial romantic friendship with Jonathan, in his magnanimous forgiveness of his enemies and Saul. He was sinner, too, adulterer, murderer.

He was a happy warrior, building a kingdom by the sword. He made Jerusalem a capital; henceforth it is "The City of David." His was a strong arm. It brought peace.

He was a king-administrator of first rank, ruling through love, priests, scribes, and elders. He knew how to wear the purple, how to grasp a scepter.

He was poet and musician, the "sweet singer of Israel," father of minstrelsy and bards. Read his Psalms. They glow like living coals.

His great career knew sin and fault and cruelty, but it was great for a' that. God so loved him that He built him a house, gave him a Messiah for a son.

*1 Samuel 18:1-II Samuel 2:12.*

# Merab

MERAB IS A CASUALTY OF ROMANCE, A SWEET VICTIM of court intrigue. She narrowly missed being wife and queen to Israel's greatest king. Whether she cared or not we are not told.

Eldest daughter of King Saul, she had been promised as a bride to any man in Saul's army who could kill Goliath. When David appeared at Saul's tent-flap with the monster's head in his hand, the promise was kept. David and Merab were to wed. Merab was willing enough. Like every other man, woman, and child in Israel, she loved the new "Captain Courageous."

But the wedding was postponed, and then forgotten. Another princess daughter in the palace, Merab's younger sister, looked on the golden-haired hero and made up her mind to have him for herself. She won, aided by Saul, who cunningly planned to use young Michal to get rid of David for good. So he married off Merab to Adriel the Meholathite. A promise meant nothing—to Saul. But what, we wonder, did it mean to Merab? Did happiness come to her with the five sons she bore to Adriel, or . . .

*I Samuel 17:25; 18:17 ff.; II Samuel 21:8.*

# Michal

MICHAL IS THE ETERNAL FEMININE, NEVER TO BE UN-
derstood. There is more wild discord in her nature than
in the swirl of a hurricane. That may be why Saul
thought he could use her.

In girlhood she was beautiful, and during her early
years with David most adorable. She dared her father's
wrath to save his life, concealing a dummy in his bed
and letting him down (Rahab-wise!) out of her window. But when he became a Palestinian Robin Hood,
outlawed by Saul, she married Phaltiel, son of Laish.
Phaltiel loved her. When David dropped the rôle of
Robin Hood and came home in triumph, he demanded
Michal back again. Phaltiel yielded, but followed Michal, in tears, to Bahurim.

Something had happened to Michal's heart while
David had been away. She had changed. She never had
understood him; now she shunned him. On that great
day when he brought the Ark back to Jerusalem, she
saw him "leaping and dancing before Jehovah," and she
condemned him mercilessly. It was the end. He never
forgave her.

*I Samuel 18:20 ff.; 19:11 ff.; 25:44; II Samuel
3:14 ff.; 6:16 ff.*

# *Abigail*

ABIGAIL MARRIED A CHURL, A DRUNKEN FOOL NAMED
Nabal. He had three thousand sheep and a thousand
goats. David, in hiding and needing food, heard about
that. Down to Nabal's shearing-pen came ten men of his
army, to beg supplies. Nabal met them with an ugly
hospitality, offering them galling insult in place of food.
David, swearing vengeance, buckled on his sword and
started for Nabal. Abigail stopped him, made him
change his mind, made him love again.

Aware of the consequences of her boorish husband's
act, she took matters into her own hands. She packed
huge bundles of food and set out for David's camp.
(Two hundred loaves, two bottles of fine wine, five
sheep, corn, raisins, and figs.) That conquered David.
He forgot Nabal and revenge.

Next morning, she told her husband. Shame and sick-
ness (alcoholism?) got hold of him. In ten days he was
dead. "And David sent and communed with Abigail, to
take her to him to wife."

A better match, this, than David and Michal. Sharp,
sensible, self-renouncing and brave, she was by far the
best of his wives. She gave him one son, Chileab.

*I Samuel 25:14 ff.; II Samuel 3:3.*

# Jonathan

SAUL'S SON AND MICHAL'S BROTHER AND BETTER THAN both of them, Jonathan gave his life in obedient sonship to his father, but reserved his heart in spontaneous affection for David. Here is friendship fit for the Kingdom of God.

His arm was steel. With an armor-bearer, he crept into a Philistine camp at night to kill twenty of them. When his father's battalions moved, Jonathan marched with the front rank. There he died, at Saul's side.

His heart was gold. He dared plead for the life of David in the face of Saul's murderous jealousy. He went secretly to warn David whenever Saul lifted his spear, warning him for the last time in the deep wilderness of Ziph; soon he was dead at bloody Gilboah. Broken, David wept: "O Jonathan . . . thy love to me was wonderful, passing the love of women. How are the mighty fallen, and the weapons of war perished!" War's weapons—and her laurels—are cheap tinsel when such a friendship is involved.

He died for his father, renounced his throne to his friend. In some ways Jonathan was more akin to Christ than David was.

*I Samuel 14:6 ff.; 18:1 ff.; 20:1 ff.; 31:2;*
*II Samuel 1:19 ff.*

# *Ahimelech*

DAVID, FLEEING FROM SAUL, MET AHIMELECH THE priest. Ahimelech knew nothing of the trouble between the harpist and the king. "Why art thou alone?" he asked the fugitive. David lied to him, saying that he was "on a secret mission for the king." He needed bread to eat, too, and a sword. Innocently, the priest supplied him, with *communion* bread and *Goliath's* sword.

Saul heard of it. Giving aid and comfort to the enemy! That was treason. Sitting "under a tree in Ramah, having his spear in his hand, and all his servants . . . standing about him," he summons the priest. A sham trial, and Ahimelech stands condemned. "Thou shalt surely die, Ahimelech, thou and all thy father's house." Eighty-five defenseless priests were butchered.

A priest caught in No-Man's Land. An innocent victim of war's madness. It was ever thus. Priests and their gods are easily shoved aside when the hell of war breaks loose. Brotherhood is laughable when bullets fly; one bursting shell can drown a thousand prayers.

It need not be always thus.

*I Samuel 21:1 ff.; 22:9 ff.*

# Doom

THERE WAS A SPY LOOKING ON WHILE AHIMELECH
gave David the shew-bread and the sword; something,
some one meaner than a spy. Doeg was a despicable
Iago, perfidious, diabolical, ready to do anything to in-
gratiate himself into Saul's favor. He ran with swift feet
as an evil wind to tell his master.

Saul, enraged, commanded his footmen to slay Ahimelech and his brother priests. They refused. "I'll do
it," cries leering Doeg. It was a task to warm his Stygian
soul. His sword flashed in the sun while Saul looked
on, until eighty-five dead bodies lay in a circle at his
feet. Even that was not enough. "And Nob, the city of
the priests, smote he . . . both men and women, children
and sucklings, and oxen, and asses, and sheep . . ."
Then he stopped.

Perhaps he had a grudge against the priests. Perhaps
he killed because he liked to kill, or just to gain promotion. Whichever be true, his heart hid the most menac-
ing of all loyalties: that doglike, slavish obedience to a
madman who happened to be king. Deaf to pity, dumb
to reason, blind to pain, it is as dangerous now as then.

*I Samuel 21:7; 22:9 ff.*

89

# *Abiathar*

ONE PRIEST ONLY GOT AWAY FROM DOEG. HE WAS
Abiathar, fourth in descent from Eli, and Ahimelech's
son.

His flight is historically important. It symbolized the
flight of all religious sympathy with Saul on the part of
the nation. Henceforth he loses popularity rapidly; he is
no longer a patriot, but a tyrant. The shadows of doom
are gathering fast.

Abiathar followed David in all his wanderings, and
was his high priest during the royal days in Hebron and
Jerusalem. He remained loyal when Absalom turned
traitor, but when Adonijah tried to seize the throne
from Solomon, Abiathar threw in his lot with the usurper. He lost his priesthood when the attempt collapsed.
Zadok, his companion under David, became the sole
high priest.

His downfall excites little sympathy. Those who take
sides in political war, high priests and laymen alike,
must expect to abide by the fortunes of war.

*I Samuel 22:20 ff.; 23:6 ff.; 30:7; II Samuel
15:29; I Kings 1:7, 19; I Kings 2:26 f.*

# *Abner*

Did we speak of the fortunes of war? Here is a man—an unimpeachable gentleman—who happened to be on the wrong side. Like Major André.

He was Saul's cousin, Saul's commander-in-chief. He it was who had led young David, bearing Goliath's head, down to the king's tent; he was sleeping at Saul's feet the night David and Abishai crawled into the trench.

With Saul dead and David proclaimed king of Judah, Abner, unswervingly loyal to Saul, proclaimed Ish-bosheth king of Israel. War followed as the night the day, between the rival kings. Israel under Abner was whipped by Judah under Joab at the "very sore battle" of Gibeon.

Abner married Rizpah, Saul's ex-concubine; idiotic Ish-bosheth reproached him for it. Incensed, the loyal officer went over to David, and in David's service was treacherously murdered by Joab. You see, Abner had been compelled, at Gibeon, in self-defense, to slay Joab's brother Asahel.

In sorrow and indignation, David mourned Abner before the people. "Know ye not that there is a prince and a great man fallen this day . . . ?" Yes, a prince and a great man—somehow on the wrong side. Or was Joab only jealous of Abner's popularity?

*I Samuel 14:51; 17:57 f.; 26:7 f.; II Samuel 2:8 ff.; 3:6 ff.*

# Joab

JOAB WAS A FIGHTING-HACK, THE MOST TALENTED AND audacious of Zeruiah's children. He was three-quarters patriot and one-quarter butcher; constancy and vindictiveness boiled in him like the red bubbling brew in a witch's pot.

He stabbed Abner to death to make himself "lord" over the armies of Israel. Give him his due. He made a good one; he was a fine general. He brought peace between David and erring Absalom, but he finished it off by killing Absalom (against David's orders). When deposed as captain for the murder, he reinstated himself immediately; he assassinated his successor!

David liked him, and David was afraid of him. Dying, he left Solomon orders to kill him. Death stalked Joab down his trail of blood. Benaiah, old friend of David, cornered him cringing against an altar in Gibeon, and finished him. Joab deserved it. By this time he was a traitor, in rebellion with Adonijah.

Victor of many a hard battle, pillar of society, patriot —that might have been his record. But in gray-headed old age he had to stain it all with cowardice, murder, and treason.

*II Samuel 2:18; 3:27; 14:1 ff.; 18:14; 19:13; 20:8 ff.; II Kings 2:5 f.; 28 ff.*

# Ish-bosheth

ISH-BOSHETH, A SON OF SAUL, WAS LEGITIMATE SUCCESSOR to the throne. His head had not the right proportions for crown-bearing. He only went through the motions; behind the throne stood Abner. Ish-bosheth was a boy born in the wrong house.

He was forty when he was set up as puppet king, and he ruled for just two years. Abner made all the decisions of state. Only once did Ish-bosheth speak up, and then he made a fool of himself. He insulted Abner over Rizpah, and Abner deserted him. When news came of Abner's death, Ish-bosheth saw the handwriting on the wall. He knew that "his hands were feeble," now, more than ever.

Don't laugh at him. The sight of him trying to ride the throne is a sight for tears, not ridicule. He is like that idiotic "King" Charles of France in Bernard Shaw's *St. Joan,* who whimpers to The Maid, "What is the good of sitting on the throne when the other fellows give all the orders? However (he sits enthroned, a piteous figure), here is a king for you. Look your fill at the poor devil."

Look your fill and try to laugh.

*II Samuel 2:8 ff.; 3:6 ff.; 4:1.*

# Uzzah

FOR TWENTY YEARS THE ARK HAD BEEN HIDDEN IN Gibeah, in the house of one Abinadab. Now King David resolved to bring it in triumph to his new Jerusalem. Accordingly, it was loaded on an ox-cart; Ahio, son of Abinadab, led the oxen, while Uzzah, his brother, walked alongside. The oxen stumbled, the Ark rocked, and Uzzah, instinctively, put up his hand to steady it. A perfectly natural and innocent gesture. He was struck dead for his pains.

Too many of us misunderstand the incident. Death struck for Uzzah not because of his rash "profanity," but because the Ark was being improperly transported. It should have been carried on the shoulders of the Levites.

It was exemplary, not personal, punishment. The nation at large had been irreverent with the Ark; they had not been seeking God "after the due order."

The triumphal procession broke up in a panic; in mortal funk, the marchers rushed the Ark into the house of Obededom and left it there.

Is it "fitting that one man should die for the people"? Does it work?

*1 Samuel 7:2; II Samuel 6:1 ff.; Numbers 4:15.*

# Mephibosheth

RISEN TO POWER, DAVID THOUGHT OFTEN OF DEAD, BE-
loved Jonathan, whose throne he sat upon. One day, in
reminiscent mood, he asked, "Is there yet any that is
left of the house of Saul, that I may show him kindness
for Jonathan's sake?" There was one—Jonathan's own
son. David sent for him. Mephibosheth!

His nurse had dropped him when he was a baby,
breaking both feet, crippling him for life; discomfort led
him forever after in chains. He found invalid's asylum
with merciful Machir-ben-Ammiel, who brought him up
and saw him married. The summons of David over-
whelmed Mephibosheth. "What is thy servant," he
stammers, "that thou shouldst look upon such a dead
dog as I am?" Crippled feet. Inferiority complex. David
was never seen in better poise. He treated Mephibosheth as his own son. He gave him Ziba, old servant of
Saul, as manservant.

Years later a dark rift separated them. Mephibosheth
turned rebel. Then he stood abject and penitent before
his benefactor, unkempt, unshaved, tattered, shifty-
eyed. He said it was all Ziba's fault. Ziba said it was his.
It makes little difference; the deep love was gone; suspicion went with them into Sheol.

*II Samuel 4:4; 9:1 ff.; 19:24 ff.*

# *Uriah*

DAVID HAD DISCIPLINE. HE HAD OFFICERS IN HIS ARMY who were men of character, men he could trust. He had Uriah, a Hittite, converted to the Jewish faith and loving this king of the Jews. Uriah married the daughter of a fellow officer, a beauty named Bath-sheba. He loved her passionately.

He went where he was sent, where duty called; no questions asked. He was fighting with Joab at the siege of Rabbah when David sent for him to come down to Jerusalem and tell him of the war. Uriah did not know that Bath-sheba was to have a child—by David—and that David was afraid.

Straight and clean he stood before a shamefaced, guilty David. He went back to camp with a sealed letter in his hand. It was his own death-warrant. "Set ye Uriah in the forefront of the hottest battle . . ." David wrote. Joab understood. Next morning Uriah fell with an arrow through his heart.

It may be best that Uriah never knew what was written in that letter; it is surely best that he never knew what his beautiful Bath-sheba had done. Or—did he know, and want to die?

*II Samuel 11:2 ff.*

# Bath-sheba

MICHAL APPEALED TO DAVID'S EYE, ABIGAIL TO HIS mind, Bath-sheba to his lust. The biographer is brutally frank about how he got her: "And David sent messengers and took her." Crude, for a king. Worse than crude, for a David.

When she conceived, they were terrified. Death was the penalty for adultery. Together they schemed to have Uriah come home, but home Uriah never came. That's why he had to die. Murder to cover adultery! As soon as he died, David and Bath-sheba married.

Their child sickened and died; so much for their punishment. She gave him four other sons: Solomon, Shimea, Shodab, Nathan, and she drew from him the promise that Solomon should succeed to the throne over his elder brother. She had power at court. She even influenced the judgments of Solomon when David was gone.

She wept when Uriah died. Was that a pose? Hers is a character hard to analyze; it is not black, not white. Just a dirty, apologetic gray.

*II Samuel 11:4; 12:15 ff.; I Chronicles 3:5;*
*I Kings 1:15 ff.*

# Nathan

DAVID ONCE THOUGHT TO BUILD A GREAT TEMPLE IN Jerusalem. He asked Nathan, the prophet, about it. Nathan first said "Yes," then "No." Both times David took his advice. Nathan spoke as one with authority.

Hearing of the king's sin with Bath-sheba, he came boldly into court, recited a little parable about a ewe lamb, a rich man and a poor one. David blazed with anger when he caught the subtle meaning of it, but even royal anger failed to halt Nathan. Gaunt and fearless, he leveled a long, terrible finger at David's eyes and shouted, "Thou art the man!" David quailed; he repented and confessed. Then he heard from the merciless Nathan three prophecies of doom as penalties for his sin: his child by Bath-sheba should die, his wives be publicly dishonored, and the sword should never leave his house. It was good prophecy; it all happened.

Gaunt Nathan is at once the inspiration and despair of all those prophets since who have allowed themselves to be chained to the chariot wheels of state, who have failed to speak for God when "royalty" has erred.

*II Samuel 7:1 ff.; 12:1 ff.*

# *Absalom*

"FROM THE SOLE OF HIS FOOT EVEN TO THE CROWN OF his head there was no blemish in him." His face hid the soul of a devil. A wolf in angel's clothes.

He killed Ammon, and hid for three years with King Talmai of Geshur. Reconciled through the efforts of Joab, it was two years more ere his father spoke to him. Meanwhile he schemed. He "stole the hearts of the men of Israel" by his princely bearing and courtesy. Then he struck, caught David unawares, and was proclaimed king at Hebron in Judah. Had he won so easily? Upset the throne without the hurling of a spear?

No; ill-advised, Absalom crossed the Jordan for an open fight. They fought in Gilead, and the enraged men of David scattered the rebels like rabbits. Absalom ran with the rest, through Ephraim's woods; a low branch caught him by the head and swung him off his mule. Joab found him hanging there and slew him.

His father loved him even as he hung dead in the tree: "Oh, Absalom, my son . . . would God I had died for thee."

The Hebrew Alcibiades!

*II Samuel 13:37 ff.; 14:25;*
*14:28; 15:6; 18:6 ff.*

# *Ahithophel*

AHITHOPHEL WAS GRANDFATHER TO BATH-SHEBA AND privy-councilor to King David. He was efficient. People thought he must have "enquired at the oracle of God." He lost faith in David.

Ahithophel joined Absalom in the rebellion. That was fortunate—for Absalom. He had a man of brains and nerve to help him. Had he followed Ahithophel's advice, he might never have died in the forest. The ex-privy-councilor, knowing that David had left Jerusalem on being advised of the "crowning" in Hebron, advised Absalom to seize the royal harem (which he did), and to attack the fleeing David at once (which he did not). Ahithophel was right: it was the logical move at that stage of the game. But he was overruled. Absalom demurred, gave David time to recover, and lost.

Then the ex-privy-councilor did another wise thing. Sensing Absalom's doom, seeing "that his counsel was not followed, he saddled his ass, and arose, and gat him to his house, to his city, and set his house in order, and hanged himself, and died."

Privy-councilor, traitor, adviser rejected, suicide! *Wise* Ahithophel? Hardly. Still, you were a more shapely traitor than Absalom.

*II Samuel 15:12; 16:20 ff.; 17:1 ff.; 21 ff.*

# Shimei

DAVID LED HIS TROOPS ONE DAY ALONG THE TOP OF A narrow hill. Up jumped a clown. Shimei, a Benjamite, came running with an armful of stones, which he hurled at the astonished column as he hurled curses at David. Jaunty Abishai begged permission to "go over . . . and take off his head." "No", said David, "let him curse." A sensible decision. Sticks and stones may break our bones, but . . .

When the tables were turned and David came home in triumph, Shimei quickly changed his mind. He threw himself at David's feet in penitential adoration. It was a good act; David was unimpressed. He was suspicious of the stone-thrower to the end. He told Solomon to watch him.

Solomon did. He ordered Shimei not to go outside the walls of Jerusalem, on pain of death. For three years Shimei obeyed. Then one day two of his slaves ran away and, child that he was, he left the city to trail them down. When he came back with them he died. Solomon was suspicious, too.

A boy's head on a man's shoulders. Were he alive now he might be stunting airplanes or sitting on flagpoles.

*II Samuel 16:5 ff.; 19:16 ff.; I Kings 2:8 ff.; 36 ff.*

# *Amasa*

CHANCE BOBBED HIM AROUND LIKE A CORK ON A WAVE. With Abigail, David's step-sister, for a mother, Amasa had the blood royal in his veins and a bright road ahead. But he chose to walk in the shadows. He deserted the king for Absalom, was appointed the rebel commander-in-chief, and staked his fortune on the dice of war. He lost. He escaped the slaughter that followed the débâcle. Now he had only a life in exile ahead.

Then chance threw her dice again, and Amasa won. Joab took the life of David's beloved, and the king, incensed, put Amasa in his place!

In the midst of another campaign Joab and Amasa met face to face. "And Joab said to Amasa, art thou in health, my brother? And Joab took Amasa by the beard with the right hand to kiss him . . ." and with his hidden left hand drove a dagger through his heart.

General for a day, then death. Who wants it?

*II Samuel 17:25; 19:13; 20:8 ff.*

# *Rizpah*

SHE HAD BEEN CONCUBINE FOR SAUL. AT HIS DEATH she lived quietly at Mahanaim with her servants and her sons.

Then a famine came to Gibeon, and she heard with bursting heart that seven sons of Saul were to be sacrificed that the anger of Jehovah might be appeased. The Gibeonites had suffered much from Saul. They would relish hanging his sons.

They hung them all on a high black hill. As they swung in the wind, frantic Rizpah came in sackcloth. (She had once graced the Court in ermine!) She sat on a rock with a stick in her hand, rose screaming now and then to drive off a carrion-hunting vulture or a wolf. From the barley harvest until the season of the rain she kept her watch, haggard, wild-eyed, tireless, dangerous as a lioness guarding her dead cubs. Some one told David. He cut the seven down, and buried them.

A barbaric religion, to demand such sacrifice; a weak David to allow it; a gallant mother in Israel, this Rizpah, keeping her vigil in rain and dark and howling storm, fighting birds and beasts of prey. Gallant, even when reason had fled.

*II Samuel 3:7; 21:7 ff.*

# Benaiah

CAPTAIN OF THE ROYAL BODYGUARD; SON OF JEHOIADA the high priest; mightiest of David's "mighty men" is Benaiah. He is the kind of war hero still done in granite for the marketplace.

He slew two "lion-like men of Moab." He went down alone into a deep dark pit on a snowy day and killed a lion. But his greatest exploit was with "the Egyptian." Nearly as big as Goliath, this fellow carried a spear as heavy as a weaver's beam. Benaiah tore it out of his hand and drove it through his midriff. *Voilà! Banzai!*

He was a faithful human watchdog for two kings— David and Solomon. He never wavered. When Adonijah tried to snatch the crown from Solomon, "Zadok the priest, and Benaiah the son of Jehoiada, and Nathan the prophet, and Shimei and Rei and the mighty men which belonged to David, were *not* with Adonijah."

As faithful as Dumas' Three Musketeers, living about the same kind of life, seeing things with the same eyes. Such men, we suppose, are necessary in such times.

*II Samuel 23:20 ff.; I Kings 1:8.*

# *Hiram*

KING HIRAM OF TYRE WAS THE MASTER BUILDER OF antiquity. Royal, loyal friend of David's and Solomon's, he helped the father build a palace and the son a temple, while he built for himself a Tyre which was the marvel-city of the world.

It was a kingdom of scattered islands, some of them a half-mile out to sea, connected by breakwaters, piers, and fortifying walls. Here he established a world trade in the famous Tyrian purple dye; from here went fleets of ships bearing explorers, traders, artisans, laborers. They had markets on the Nile, worked copper-mines in Crete and Cyprus, built colonies in Malta and Sicily, mined gold in Spain and tin in Cornwall. Wise Solomon joined hands with wise Hiram; Jewish ships sailed the waves manned by Tyrian seamen. Together they lifted their kingdoms to the heights of their earthly glory in the piping times of peace. When they died and warriors came to rule again, the kingdoms faded away. Over once-glorious Tyre ran the armies of Shalmanezer, Sennacherib, Ashurbanipal, Nebuchadnezzar, Artaxerxes, and Alexander; they left a village of huts where the waves pound now on the ruins of her lost magnificence.

*II Samuel 5:11; I Kings 5:1 ff.; 9:26 ff.*

# *Adonijah*

ADONIJAH EXPECTED TO BE KING. HE HAD EVERY RIGHT to expect it. He was the eldest son of dying David, the next in line, the heir apparent. He held a great banquet under the trees; his banqueters shouted "Long live King Adonijah." They shouted too soon.

At the palace Bath-sheba was plotting as the old king breathed his last. She wanted that throne for her son Solomon. With Nathan's aid she wheedled a promise from David that Solomon should be king. His choice stood; the son of Bath-sheba took the throne. Adonijah was "pardoned" on condition that he "show him a worthy man"!

But artful Bath-sheba still feared his influence, his popularity. That story of Adonijah asking for Abishag was probably her invention. Surely he must have known that such a request would be considered a threat at the throne, and that death would be the penalty. Death was the penalty—Benaiah was sent to kill him.

His battered life and cruel death, both undeserved, must rouse sympathy in the heart of a stone.

Solomon the Wise, Temple-builder and ruthless absolutist, is king.

*1 Kings 5 ff.; 2:13 ff.*

# *Solomon*

He glitters with bigness—and it hides him. Solomon was not big. He lifted his kingdom high only to give it a greater fall.

His "great Temple" was no larger than our ordinary church; he had a thousand wives and a thousand foreign, contaminating gods; 12,000 horsemen and 1,400 chariots; palaces, fortresses, fleets. To build them he virtually enslaved his people in forced labor. To pay his intolerable taxes they lived in hovels and starvation; he never lifted his finger to help them. They groaned; he called for more cedar palaces, more golden drinking-cups.

Wise? He had a mind essentially selfish and unsound. He squandered a great inheritance and left a kingdom disintegrating, rebellious, seething with discontent. Egotist, sensualist, tyrant, he died without honor or regret.

His writings give him away. (Solomon wrote three thousand proverbs, and his Songs were a thousand and five.) His Songs reveal him in the days of his youthful innocence, his Proverbs in the days of his wisdom and moral strength, his Ecclesiastes in the days of his bitter, aged disenchantment. "All is vanity" is his Great Amen.

Men need more than Lebanon cedars to build a lasting kingdom. They need God.

*I Kings 1-11; 4:32; 10:26; 11:3;*
*II Chronicles 1-9.*

# Queen of Sheba

SHE CAME FROM RADIANT ARABIA, WHERE MARBLE palaces basked amid gardens delectable, where fine old trees defeated the fierce sun and great dikes watered wide green pastures; the air was so sparklingly pure that everyone lived long.

She heard the wild tales of Solomon's splendor—a splendor rivaling hers. Her imagination captivated, she loaded a caravan with treasure and went to see for herself. She would match his silver and his gold and his wit!

He was too much for her. His treasure-vaults made her feel poor; he answered every riddle she could think of. (Did this riddle-answering make people think him wise?) They exchanged gifts and she went home. A long trip, just to match coins and answer riddles. Maybe she had an alliance, political or commercial, in mind.

Countless legends are woven about her visit, most of them just legends. One of the most persistent is that she had a son by Solomon; the Abyssinians of today boast that their royal line descended from him. Why boast?

But to be honest with her, she had the spirit of adventure, a brilliant, inquiring mind, a craving for fellowship, and no envy whatsoever.

*I Kings 10:1 ff.*

# Rezon

OLD WAR-DOG, OLD HAND AT MUTINY, WAS REZON OF Damascus. He was no Hadad, with a deep love for his native soil. He was just a natural guerilla-fighter and trouble-maker.

Back in David's time he had fought under the banners of Hadadezer the Syrian. When the Syrians "became servants to David and brought gifts," Rezon deserted to lead a band of freebooters in the wilderness. Gathering strength, they struck at the city of Damascus, took it, ruled it, fortified it, made it a hornet's nest in Solomon's back yard.

Rezon and his men were never dangerous adversaries. Just bothersome. They started their mischief at the very beginning of Solomon's reign, and they were at it when he died. With Hadad to the south of him and Rezon to the north of him and a harem of a thousand right at home, King Solomon was tasting vinegar in his golden drinking-cup.

Some fight for medals, some for land, and some, like Rezon, fight for fun.

*II Samuel 8:6; I Kings 11:23 ff.*

# *Ahijah*

SOLOMON FEASTED WHILE HIS KINGDOM CRACKED. AGE
and vanity blinded him. He could not see what Ahijah,
prophet of Shiloh, saw.

Ahijah met a strong young man in a beautiful cloak;
he ripped it from his shoulders, tore it into twelve small
pieces, gave ten of them to the young man with some
good advice: ". . . thus saith the Lord, the God of
Israel, behold I will rend the kingdom out of the hand
of Solomon, and will give ten tribes to thee . . . if thou
wilt hearken unto all that I command thee . . . and do
that which is right in my sight . . . I will be with thee,
and build thee a sure house . . ." The sure house was
never built. The strong young man (Jeroboam) took
the ten pieces and the ten tribes but not the good
advice.

A kingdom tumbling! A lonely prophet seeing it and
planning with God against its stern tomorrow! A head-
strong youth who made the planning vain! Prophets
often read the signs of the times aright, while rulers play
and priests stand blindly by.

Jeroboam and the prophet never met again; but Ahijah foretold the death of his son, the destruction of his
house.

*I Kings 11:29 ff.; 14:1 ff.*

# *Jeroboam*

HE SPLIT A NATION AND A NATION'S FAITH. HE WAS THE
first king of the divided kingdom of Israel, the first of
nineteen sovereigns who ruled two hundred and fifty
years and among whom was not one godly man.

He was Solomon's Secretary of Labor and Taxes
when he met Ahijah. He tried rebellion and failed and
fled to Egypt, where he married into the royal house.

The minute Solomon was dead he came back, back
this time as king of the ten northern tribes, back as
Lord of Misrule. He erected a pair of golden calves for
his kingdom to worship; he was reproved and pardoned
and spared to sin again. He went to war with Judah,
and remained at war until his heart broke at the loss of
an army of five hundred thousand men. Then he died.

He could lead; he was not mediocre in any sense. His
fatal weakness was that he subordinated religious faith
and zeal to political ambition. He led Israel in the worship of false gods; he helped a nation to lose its soul. He
set no value on God's favor; God set no value on him.

*I Kings 11:26 ff.; 12:1-14:20.*

# Rehoboam

SOLOMON BEGAT A SIMPLETON AND CALLED HIM RE-
hoboam. Ascending the throne on his father's demise,
he received a large delegation from the people, headed
by Jeroboam, asking relief from forced labor and taxes.
(Shorter hours and more pay!) His elderly advisers,
fearful of the coming storm, advised him to comply and
lighten the people's load. But his younger advisers (always more intolerant and severe) advised him to
reprimand the malcontents, which he did: "My father
chastised you with whips, but I will chastise you with
scorpions." It was the last straw. "To your tents, O
Israel," was the answer of the ten revolting tribes. Rehoboam fled to Jerusalem, king now of only Judah and
Benjamin. Even these, under his management, knew
naught but decline.

Overnight, as time goes, Solomon's glory was gone.
His Temple was stripped to buy off Shishak of Egypt,
who captured Jerusalem easily five years later. The son
took up the worst sins of his father, and died not soon
enough. His greatest achievement was that he had eighteen wives, sixty concubines, twenty-eight sons and sixty
daughters.

Revolutions never come because of what the people
want. They come because of what the rulers are.

*I Kings 12:1 ff.; 14:21 ff.; II Chronicles 11:21.*

# *Adoniram*

PSYCHOLOGISTS CALL IT THE MARTYR COMPLEX; CYNICS call it stupidity. One label is as good as another. Most of us have it. Humanity will ever be remarkable for the amount of punishment it can take.

Adoniram had the most unpopular occupation in the world, and he liked it well enough to hold it for better than fifty years. He was tax-collector, or "receiver of the tribute," for David, Solomon, and Rehoboam. Under David it was hard enough; under Solomon he feared for his life; under Rehoboam he lost it.

He knew what that "whips of scorpions" speech of Rehoboam's meant; he knew, the day the king sent him into Israel to collect the oppressive tax, that violence would greet him. Yet he went, ". . . and all Israel stoned him with stones, that he died." Rehoboam saved his skin by flight while the old tribute-taker died.

Is this loyalty or foolishness? *Should* one die for a Rehoboam? *Should* the Tory Adonirams who collected the stamp tax for Rehoboamish George III have quit their king and joined the popular party—or was their cause worth standing for, even when the day was lost?

*II Samuel 20:24; I Kings 4:6; 12:18.*

# Abijah

REHOBOAM'S SON WAS JUDAH'S SECOND KING. IN BETTER
times he might have had a better time. His day was too
much for him. In an hour of revolution he tried to call
the people back to the order of things they had revolted
against; naturally, he failed.

From the top of a mountain he exhorted the men of
Jeroboam: "Ought ye not to know that the Lord God of
Israel gave the kingdom over Israel to David forever . . . ?" A Fourth of July oration, with appropriate
gestures. It fell flat. The people were sick of such bom-
bast, already beginning to understand that God gives his
kingdoms to those who can take care of them, not to
those who just want them.

A failure at oratory, Abijah turned to arms and won.
He trounced Jeroboam soundly, and took cities in Israel
away from him. But it was useless. Soon Abijah
"walked in all the sins of his father." Soon he died. His
was one of the last futile attempts to recover the Ten
Tribes.

*1 Kings 15:1 ff.; II Chronicles 13:1 ff.*

# *Asa*

ONE NEVER KNOWS ABOUT HEREDITY. SAINTS BREED devils, and devils saints. Brothers may be opposites. Abijah was bad and his brother (?) Asa was one of Judah's fairest kings.

He loved to smash idols. Right and left he swung at Baal and Asherah, while he hounded their devotees. He was merciless against the enemies of Jehovah, even in his own house. He deposed the Queen mother for idolatry! Religiously, he swept the kingdom clean.

Politically, he was an opportunist. He defeated Zerah the Ethiopian and came home with "very much spoil." He did not keep it long. Baasha of Israel harried him in a sniper's war, and Asa sent for Benhadad of Syria to help him. He had to empty the Temple of its treasures to pay for it—but he stopped Baasha. Treasure? Dangerous alliance? They meant nothing!

In his old age he suffered kingly pain: Asa had the gout.

He was loved and honored. He never walked in his father's sins. "The good king Asa" reigned forty-one years. Judged against his day, he was phenomenal.

*1 Kings 15:9 ff.; II Chronicles 14:1-16:14.*

# Baasha

BAASHA SWAM TO POWER DOWN A RIVER OF BLOOD. Son of Ahijah of the tribe of Issachar, he conspired against Nadab (Jeroboam's son and successor) and slew him. He slew the whole house of Jeroboam as a farmer slays his swine; he "left not to Jeroboam any that breathed . . ." Long live King Baasha!

Once in control, he widened his red river; he waged continual war with Asa the Southerner. He fortified Ramah (near Jerusalem) to cut off all communication with Judah. But he woke up one morning to hear that Benhadad was laying waste the far-off towns of Ijon and Dan. A new threat! Abandoning Ramah, he marched toward the Syrian—and the Syrian marched toward home, without a battle. While Baasha was away on his wild-goose chase, Asa swept down on Ramah and demolished it. Brains had conquered brawn.

Baasha walked in all the follies of Jeroboam. He held on for twenty-four years and then he died.

Some men live, some exist.

*1 Kings 15:27 ff.; 1 Chronicles 16:1 ff.*

# Jehoshaphat

IT IS INCREDIBLE. IMPOSSIBLE. IT HAPPENED. JEHOSHA-
phat, Judah's third ruler, was an improvement on his father, Asa.

He had a wider, deeper piety. Not only did he smash
Baal's idols, but he sent out his own home missionaries,
itinerant preachers, to instruct the nation in Jehovah's
morality and religion. He was constructive.

He was a wiser builder. Under him prosperity returned, commerce revived, riches and honors flowed
back.

He was a better soldier. He not only strengthened his
home defenses, but he awed Ammon, Edom, and
Moab. He made an alliance with Israel. Had Israel been
blessed then with a kingly king, the United Kingdom
might have been reborn. His troops sang as they fought.
They had morale.

He reorganized his courts, separated church and
state, gave swift and impartial administration of justice.
His one great mistake was that good-intentioned alliance with Ahab, his easy compliance with Ahab's low
scheming. But it is significant that even the prophets,
who watched him closest, rebuked him little and loved
him much. He was one of the few really fit to be king.

*I Kings 15:24; 22:41 ff.; II Chronicles 17:1-21:1.*

# *Zimri*

ZIMRI RULED JUST SEVEN DAYS. HE NEVER FAIRLY GOT hold of the crown.

It may be honorable to kill a degenerate, but what about killing, without reason or need, all the relatives of the degenerate? When the army before Gibbethon heard of what Zimri had done, heard of the rivers of blood in the palace at Tirzah, they revolted, lifted the siege, and marched on Zimri.

The Pretender dared not risk a pitched battle; he defended the city. It was short. His barricades went down like cardboard before the enraged patriots. As they swept over the last broken wall, Zimri backed into his palace. Brave and bellowing and obstinate to the bitter end, he locked the palace gate, placed his crown on his head, set his house on fire. He died in the flames; that was easier than facing the troops outside.

And in those seven days he found time to "walk in the way of Jeroboam." The perfect finishing touch for a reckless desperado. He took his chances and his punishment without a whimper.

*1 Kings 16:15 ff.*

# Omri

It was General Omri who led the attack on Zimri, who plucked the crown from the hot ashes of Tirzah and wore it himself. He was more general than king; battles absorbed him.

He had a war on his hands at the very start. "Half the people" wanted Tibni as king; the army voted for Omri. The army won—after four years of civil war. With that over, Omri built Samaria.

Samaria was an ideal choice for a new capital, a city set on a hill amid a circle of hills, dominating, beautiful, fertile, serene. It fell in time to Syria. Omri's campaigns against foreigners were more successful than his campaigns at home.

His record religiously was weak and bad. He chastened the prophets; he wanted room for sin in his house of faith. While he never sponsored heathen cults or manners, he sponsored the system of Jeroboam, which was nearly as bad.

A vigorous and unscrupulous ruler, he strengthened his dynasty by an alliance with Phœnicia, which was in time cemented by the marriage of Ahab and Jezebel. The crack of doom was in their wedding bells.

*I Kings 16:21 ff.; Micah 6:16.*

# *Ahab*

FAMOUS AND INFAMOUS. CYNIC AND PENITENT. BULLY and truckling. Sulky. Envious. Effeminate. Inconsequent. Omri's son. *Ahab!*

He ". . . did that which was evil . . . above all that were before him. . . ." Marrying Jezebel, princess of Tyre, to gain material and political advantage, he soon bowed to her like a craven, spineless slave. She was ruler, not he. He built her temples to her fiendish Baal Melkarth and her lewd Astarte; he saw the faith of his fathers all but wiped out as her imported priests and warriors ravaged Israel. He built himself a house of ivory and filled it with Tyrian purple and gold. He sold out cheaper than Judas.

Yet he was a man in battle. Three times he bested Benhadad, once even taking him prisoner. In the final fray he entered the lists as a private soldier. An arrow found him. He stood upright in his chariot, watching the ebb of battle till he died. Dogs licked up his blood, as Elijah said they would.

He was always a coward in a moral crisis. He never had a mind of his own. He threw not only his body but his life and his people to the dogs.

*I Kings 16:29 ff.; 20:1 ff.; 22:29 ff.*

# Jezebel

HAUGHTY OF BEARING; UNCONQUERABLE OF WILL; RE-
ligious fanatic; antiquity's Lady Macbeth—*Jezebel!*

She forced on Israel her Phœnician culture and her
gods. At her tables sat four hundred and fifty prophets
of Baal, four hundred of Astarte; by sword and lance
she forced all but seven thousand of the men of Israel to
their knees. All save one of the prophets of Israel she
forced into hiding—and Elijah more than once ran
from her fury.

On her fell Jehovah's curse, "The dogs shall eat Jezebel." Fourteen years after Ahab's death she heard that
Jehu was coming to slay her. She dressed, painted, per-
fumed herself as though for a court ball; she sat quietly
in her chamber window and waited. As Jehu's chariot
clattered to a halt in the street below, she taunted him,
laughed in his face. Two eunuchs threw her from the
window. Jehu drove his chariot over her broken body.
The dogs came.

She was wicked. She was vile. She was the worst
woman ever born. But she was Queen. Israel hated her,
but she ruled Israel with an iron hand. Even on that last
day, over sixty, taunting Jehu, she was Queen.

*1 Kings 18:19; 19:18; 21:23; II Kings 9:30 ff.*

# *Elijah*

HUGE AND SHAGGY, STOUT-HEARTED, THUNDER-VOICED. Lone wolf of the Lord. Israel's greatest son—*Elijah the Tishbite*.

He came from nowhere, long hair down his back, girdle of skin about his loins, to call Ahab to account, to prophesy a three-years drought. Then he hid from the enraged king (and queen) near the brook Cherith, where ravens fed him.

He leaped from hiding again to challenge the priests of Baal to an ordeal of fire on Carmel, to win it, to slay them, to hide once more. Jezebel thought he was dead. But he returned to prophesy her death. When she and Ahab were gone he rebuked their son and predicted *his* death; he did the same for wicked Jehoram.

Then he left the earth. Casting his mantle to Elisha, he ascended into heaven in a chariot of flame. He left as he had come, as he had lived, in a whirlwind of heavenly fire. He came back, at the transfiguration of our Lord.

He stood alone. He outwitted Jezebel and her priests. He destroyed Baal-worship, punished the apostate kings who introduced it, made Israel cry again, "Jehovah, He *is* God."

*I Kings 17:1-19:21; 21:17 ff.; II Kings 1:1 ff.;*
*II Kings 2:11 ff.; II Chronicles 21:11 ff.*

# Elisha

ELIJAH SAW HIM PLOWING IN A FIELD, AND CALLED him. He left his home and friends to be the Tishbite's companion, pupil, and successor. No two men were ever more different.

Elisha was a city man, with a house in Samaria. He was well groomed and mannered, more of a teacher and preacher than a prophet. He was the honored mouthpiece of the Almighty at the courts of six kings. Three called him friend; to them he was worth more than a thousand generals.

Miracles without number are credited to him. He purified pottage and water and multiplied loaves; he caused an iron ax to swim; he cured Naaman of leprosy and put it as a curse upon Gehazi; he brought a dead boy back to life; even in the tomb his bones restored the dead.

But the miracles were the least of his spiritual works. He anticipated, more than Elijah, the spirit of Jesus Christ. Elijah was wrapped in a tempest, Elisha in an aura of profoundest spiritual truth. He was God's lighthouse, steady and bright against a gay, carefree Court. In the darkest days, when doom was certain, he was still witness for truth and righteousness.

*I Kings 19:19 ff.; II Kings 2:12-13:21.*

# Jehoram of Israel

JEHORAM FOLLOWED AHAZIAH AS KING. UNSTABLE, lacking genuine religious conviction, dominated by the Queen-mother Jezebel, he was less a leader in his time than Benhadad or Hazael.

He began with what seemed to be a religious reformation. He put away the pillar of Baal everywhere, but Jezebel soon took care of *that*. She made him compromise; he condemned Baal in public, but connived at his worship in private. And that was the end of that.

He lived and died in armor. In league with Jehoshaphat, he fought Moab. He could never quite win.

Twice he fought Benhadad; twice Elisha saved him. In the first engagement the prophet snared the Syrian army and gave advice as to its treatment which won peace. In the second, Samaria was besieged. Famine raged; mothers ate their children. A miracle of providence saved the city.

Fighting at Ramoth-gilead, Jehoram was wounded. Bleeding, he retired to Jezreel. The army revolted in his absence; Elisha anointed Jehu king. Jehoram's sins had forfeited his crown. Jehu rode swiftly to Jezreel and shot Jehoram (through the back) in Naboth's garden!

He was the last of the house of Omri.

*II Kings 1:17; 3:1 ff.; 6:8-7:20; 9:1 ff.*

# Jehoram of Judah

JEHORAM OF ISRAEL WAS A SAINT COMPARED WITH Jehoram of Judah. He of Judah was Jehoshaphat's son; he murdered his six brothers. He invaded Edom to put down rebellion, and ended by acknowledging their independence. Libna also revolted and joined the Philistines. Finally Philistines on the southwest, and Arabians on the south and southeast, invaded Judah; they carried off the king's treasure and his wives and sons as prisoners. Judah was degraded; the house of David was threatened with extinction.

He married Athaliah, daughter of Ahab and the reincarnation of Jezebel. Like her mother, she ruled her king. Through her Baal was exalted in Judah; temples and orgies and high-place worship abounded.

Avaricious, bloody, and idolatrous, he passed on at forty, unwept, unhonored, and unsung. He was *not* buried in the sepulchers of the kings; he had not even the usual honor of a public funeral. Jehoram's was one of the darkest and most unfortunate reigns in the entire course of Judean history.

*II Kings 8:16 ff.; II Chronicles 21:1 ff.*

# *Jehu*

TWIN REVOLUTIONS DROVE BAAL FROM ISRAEL. ONE worked subtly, quietly, through the preaching of Elijah and the teaching of Elisha. The other worked quickly, violently, through the fury of Jehu, founder of Israel's most important, powerful, and longest-lived dynasty. He is the world's leading charioteer. He drove furiously; the hoofs of his horses dripped red blood. All revolutions before him were sham battles; all murderers, amateurs.

Anointed king, he immediately assassinated King Jehoram of Israel and seventy princes of Samaria, Ahaziah of Judah and forty-two of his kinsmen, aged Jezebel in Jezreel. He gathered all the Baalites he could find into one great temple and massacred them, removing at a single blow the whole heathen population of the kingdom.

It was all as indefensible as it was disastrous. He had no honest enthusiasm for God; ox-worship persisted, though Baal was dead. As a ruler he was useless; his wholesale slaughterings left the kingdom weak, and ere he died he was paying tribute to a new kingdom on the Euphrates. The shadow of Assyria lay full across the land.

*II Kings 9:1-10:36.*

# *Athaliah*

ATHALIAH, DAUGHTER OF AHAB AND JEZEBEL, WIFE OF
Jehoram of Judah and mother of Ahaziah, moved fast
when Jehu killed her son. She "arose and destroyed all
the seed royal." She said to Judah, "Now I'm queen."
She meant it.

Judah winced. To be ruled by a woman! And a
foreign woman at that, half Phœnician, half Israelite!
They were shocked . . . and terrified. Athaliah broke
them on the wheel of her unflinching will. For six years
she did as she pleased with them.

She pushed Baal to the fore in Judah. She did not
persecute; she built altars. The Temple of Solomon de-
cayed; the temples of Baal increased and magnified.

Athaliah was tricked. She thought she had accounted
for *all* the seed royal; she missed one baby, Joash.
Snatched from the massacre by his aunt Jehosheba, he
was hidden for six years in the Temple. One morning
Athaliah heard a shouting in her courtyard: "Long live
the king." Before the people stood Joash! She cried
loudly: "Treason! Treason!" She was dead within an
hour.

She was bold and bad, like her mother. And like her
mother, she was queen.

*II Kings 11:1 ff.*

# *Naaman*

SYRIAN NAAMAN HAD GREAT STRENGTH, THE POISE OF A patrician, the position of ranking noble at the court of Benhadad II. He was Syria's Lord Wellington. But beneath his jeweled turban and silken robe he was a leper. White leprosy, never cured!

A captive maid in his household said there was a prophet in Israel able to cure that. Grasping at the straw, the proud Syrian drove post-haste to the door of the house of Elisha. Elisha insulted him (he did not even come out to look at him!) and cured him. ("Go and wash in the Jordan seven times.") Naaman, piqued but still grasping, obeyed. And "he was clean."

Then he tried to pay Elisha. How many of us still cherish a heathen ignorance of the true function and character of true prophets! Finding that he could not pay, Naaman promised to pray. Thereafter there was no God for Naaman but Elisha's God. Thereafter, whenever he went with Benhadad to the Temple of Rimmon, Naaman prayed to Jehovah!

Naaman the leper lives on. On the traditional site of his house in Damascus is a leper hospital.

*II Kings 5:1 ff.*

# Jehoiada

JEHOSHEBA SAVED JOASH, THE HEIR-APPARENT, AND Jehoiada, her high-priest husband, guarded him. He set the sentries at the Temple-door, organized the inner bodyguard, gathered the Levites, armed the remaining loyal troops with weapons, once used by David, from the Temple armory. He placed the crown on Joash's brow.

Then he played to Joash the part that Abner had played to Ish-bosheth; he pulled the strings behind the throne. He inflamed the populace against Baalism, razed temples and smashed idols and put the old-time religion once more in control. He repaired the crumbling walls of the Temple of the Lord; carpenters, masons, builders, worked in a new frenzy of joy. The priests and Levites went to work again, the services of sacrifice and music were reëstablished. It was a great day for Judah—and for Judah's God.

When he died they gave him a great funeral and a distinction never accorded to any other subject in the history of the monarchy—High-priest Jehoiada sleeps in the city of David, in the sepulchers of the kings.

Jehoiada was wasted. The boy king he hid in the Temple never grew up.

*II Kings 11:1 ff.; 12:1 ff.; II Chronicles 24:1 ff.*

# Joash of Judah

JOASH DEPENDED TOO MUCH ON JEHOIADA. WHEN THE old high priest died, the boy went to pieces. He was a lamb among wolves, a leaner without a prop.

Bewildered, he chose as his new advisers "the princes of Judah"—the scions of the Jewish aristocracy. There was not a sound spine in the lot of them. They flattered the boy with soft, pretty speech; they led him to compromise, to toleration and restoration of Baal. When the people rebelled, he took their leader and stoned him to death. At the very Temple court he stoned priest Zechariah, son of the man who had secreted him in the Temple and made him king!

The same year, Hazael of Syria came up against Jerusalem. Joash made a feeble effort to stop him; defeated, he sent out as tribute the treasures of palace and Temple. Hazael went home gloating; Joash, humiliated and disgraced, went to bed. He was sick. There, in his sick-bed at the fortress of Millo, two of his servants killed him.

The halo of youthful romance fit him well. The crown of kingly responsibility—who measured him for that?

*II Kings 12:17 ff.; II Chronicles 24:17 ff.*

# Jehoahaz of Israel

KING JEHOAHAZ, SON OF JEHU, FELL HEIR TO LITTLE BUT trouble. The Syrian war was raging when he followed his father; Hazael had become God's scourge to punish Israel. Hazael did his work well. Savagery in his warfare reached the ultimate. ". . . the strongholds were set on fire . . . the young men were slain with the sword; the innocent children were seized and dashed to the ground; the women great with child were ripped up and brutally slaughtered." Israel was paying. So fully was her strength drained that Jehoahaz was reduced at last to ten war chariots, fifty horsemen, ten thousand infantry.

As a last hope he tried repentance. He "besought the Lord." God was not fooled. Jehoahaz was faking. He never changed his ways, never for a minute stopped his sinning. The carnage went on; the scourge was still gathering toll when Jehoahaz died.

He was no fighter, no king, no leader. He was nothing but a royal dummy rolling before the storm.

*II Kings 13:1 ff.*

# Joash of Israel

JEHU WOULD HAVE LOVED THIS GRANDSON. JOASH WAS superior to his father, Jehoahaz, indeed to most of the monarchs of Israel. True, "he departed not from all the sins of Jeroboam," but he discovered his country prostrate and bleeding and he left her independent and respected.

More God-fearing, keener-witted and sensitive than his fathers, he went early to talk with Elisha, ninety now and dying. Elisha ordered him to take arrows from his quiver and shoot them from his chamber window toward Syria. Once, twice, thrice he twanged the string. Elisha was angry when he stopped there, for the number of arrows was the number of times he was to "smite the Syrians in Aphek." He smote them. Thrice. At or near Aphek. He recovered every city west of Jordan.

King Amaziah dared him to fight Judah. He fought and won, took Amaziah captive back to his own Jerusalem, humbled Jerusalem, leveled part of her wall, went home with treasure and hostages. He left a dazed Amaziah, sadder but wiser, on a broken-legged throne.

Then he died.

*II Kings 13:10 ff.; II Chronicles 25:17 ff.*

# *Amaziah*

THE MURDER OF JOASH OF JUDAH WAS AVENGED IM-
mediately by Amaziah, his son. In his vengeance was an
innovation. He might have slain the conspirators *and*
their sons; he punished only the guilty.

Amaziah mastered Edom. With an army of three
hundred thousand he met them in the "Valley of Salt"
and put thousands of them to the sword. The eagle of
Edom was caged, her wings and talons clipped.

To make that victory sure, Amaziah hired an army of
Israelitish mercenaries. Then he fired them. Stung, they
vented their spleen by petty plundering as they went
home. It was a good excuse for a war. Arrogant in his
victory over Edom, Amaziah sent his ill-timed challenge
to Joash. The rest is history.

He reigned for fifteen years after his humbling, but he
went to war no more. All the fight had been knocked
out of him. His subjects despised him; their disgust increased when he began bowing to foreign gods. They finally killed him at Lachish, brought back his body in
the royal chariot, put it away in the royal tomb.

*II Kings 14:1 ff.; II Chronicles 25:1 ff.*

# Jeroboam II

THE REIGN OF JEROBOAM II WAS A REPRODUCTION OF the reign of Solomon. Prosperity, fickle goddess, smiled again on Israel. A Mona Lisa smile!

He won three great wars. He humbled Syria of Damascus, recovering from her the entire Trans-Jordanic region, and invaded the Damascene kingdom itself. He marched on Hamath (two hundred miles away) and reduced it after an independence of a century and a half. He subdued Ammon and Moab and established himself in the southeast.

Secure from his ancient enemies, he thrived. Rich crops leaped up, commerce revived, the arts flourished. Each man sat again beneath his vine and fig tree, drinking wine, growing lazy, selfish, fat. Stealthily as a June breeze, comfortable prosperity passed into debauchery and excess. Morals became effeminate; domestic chastity and the estate of woman declined. Heathenism got a foothold again. The prophets raged. Read Amos. Read Hosea. Jeroboam, old and deaf, let it go on.

He reigned longer than any other Israelitish king, did more than any other to increase the glory and prestige of his realm. But, like Solomon, he left it tottering. He died in the nick o' time. After him, the deluge.

*II Kings 14:23 ff.; Amos 4:1; Hosea 6:1 ff.*

# *Uzziah*

UZZIAH, AT SIXTEEN, FOLLOWED HIS FATHER AS KING. He was a popular choice: "All the people of Judah . . ." wanted him. He was true to their confidence. His reign was the finest since Solomon's.

Abroad, he conquered Edom, Ammon, Philistia, the Arabs, and restored the lucrative Red Sea trade which had made Solomon rich. At home, he was wise, vigilant, and active. He strengthened Jerusalem with new battle-towers and machinery; he led a fine army of "mighty men"; he encouraged agriculture; in the hills he had many a husband-man and vine-dresser, many a flock of sheep.

He never deserted God! That was a virtue among the kings. Perhaps he overdid it. In a bad moment, intent on self-exaltation and puffed with pride, he pushed the priests aside to offer incense himself. For that he was stricken with leprosy. As a leper he died, isolated in his palace, isolated even in death in a tomb of his own. Jotham was ruling before he died.

But for that one act of trespass in the priests' domain he would have been peerless.

*II Kings 15:1 ff.; II Chronicles 26:1 ff.*

# Jotham

JUDAH WATCHED THE DYING OF UZZIAH WITH GRAVE misgivings. This son of his . . . this Jotham . . . a good fellow, all right, but . . . no Uzziah.

He aped his father. Lacking Uzziah's strength and energy, he simply trod in the footsteps of the dead. He built a few castles and towers, dabbled in agriculture, fought one war (with the Ammonites) and won it. The same thing now was wrong in Judah that had been wrong under Jeroboam in Israel: prosperity had ruined them both.

Religion became an empty show, a vain prayer-muttering. Men got up early to be drunk longer. The princes were "rebellious and the companions of thieves." Love of gaudy dress and toilet was a mania. Soothsayers and magicians thrived. One half of Judah was heart-sick and alarmed; the other half, potvaliant and blind. And Judah lay right in the path of onrushing Tiglath-pileser, that Assyrian who was beginning to gather in, one by one, the nations of the west.

At forty-one, good-fellow Jotham died a natural death. The only natural thing, apparently, he ever did.

*II Kings 15:32 ff.; II Chronicles 27:1 ff.;
Isaiah 1:23.*

# *Pekah*

PEKAH, THE SON OF REMALIAH, AT THE HEAD OF A BAND of fifty Gileadite desperadoes, killed King Pekahiah in his harem.

Pekah was an assassin and a usurper . . . and the one man in his kingdom with sufficient military and diplomatic intelligence to ward off for fourteen years more the collapse of the state. He formed an alliance with Rezin of Damascus and marched with him on King Ahaz of Judah. Ahaz, frightened out of his senses, begged Tiglath-pileser (Pul) to come to his assistance, offering Judah as an Assyrian feudatory as reward. Pul came on the double-quick. He penned up Rezin in Damascus, captured him, and then—turned on Pekah!

Pekah was already beaten. Internal treachery, idolatry, and immorality had weakened him; Hoshea, a pretender, plotted against him from within the walls of Samaria, while outside, Pul stood at his gates. It ended by Hoshea slaying Pekah.

Pul had done well. He now had two new kingdoms in his bag. Pekah had played a bold game and lost it. Honor him only for his gallant stand against the inevitable.

*II Kings 15:23-16:9.*

# Pul

PEKAH'S NEMESIS HAD TWO NAMES. IN BABYLON HE WAS Pul; in Assyria, Tiglath-pileser IV. Either name was a synonym for holocaust.

He performed a miracle in regeneration with a run-down Assyria, making it a world power; in rapid succession he gained victories over the Aramaean tribes, over Sarduris II of Ararat, Rezin of Damascus, Hiram of Tyre, Pisiris of Carchemish. He took cities from the Medes, left them filled with bas-reliefs of his own image. He ravaged Mesopotamia, Philistia, Damascus, and Israel, made a vassal of Samsi, queen of the Arabians. Mitinti of Ashkelon, seeing the fate of Rezin, went stark mad; Rukipti, his son, and Metenna of Tyre paid him heavy tribute. In 729 B.C. he captured Ukin-zer, a Chaldean prince who had usurped the Babylonian throne; in 728 Pul himself sat on that throne; in 727 he died.

In his wake were fear, desolation, and bas-reliefs. Everywhere he left behind him slabs of stone carved with the annals and achievements of his reign. Pul liked Pul. "I took five hundred and ninety-one cities," he says. "Over sixteen districts of Syria I swept, like a flood." Only this, and nothing more, *ad infinitum*.

*II Kings 15:19, 29; 16:7 ff.*

138

# Ahaz

TOTAL DEPRAVITY HAD A BELOVED DISCIPLE IN AHAZ, Jotham's son. He was the meanest of all Judah's princes. No courage, no honor, no patriotism, energy, reverence, heart, mind nor soul.

When the cordon of his enemies began to encircle Jerusalem, he put his trust in everyone and everything but God. With never a thought of the honor of his people or his royal line, he went begging for help from Tiglath-pileser; from that hour his people were vassals and he was a vassal king.

He strangled the faith of his fathers, let religion die by inches. He offered his own son to Moloch; he was the inspiration of the realm's superstition; he talked with ghosts, wizards, and soothsayers; at the Temple gate were chariots and "sacred" white horses dedicated to the sun. First he desecrated every stick of furniture in the Temple; lastly he closed and locked the Temple doors and ordered the ancient lamps put out.

Lights out! God was gone. Vision was dead, the people perishing. Hezekiah might postpone it, but he could not stop it. Judah was doomed.

*II Kings 16:1 ff.; II Chronicles 28:1 ff.*

# *Hoshea*

THE USURPER HOSHEA, KILLER OF PEKAH, IS THE LAST
king of Samaria. He is the frustrated hero of the tragi-
comedy, pompously strutting the stage after the villain
has won. He is not responsible for his country's ruin.
That had all been arranged before he was born.

Tiglath-pileser made him, put him on the Samaritan
throne when Pekah passed. When Tiglath-pileser died,
Hoshea was done. His support, his defender, was gone.
In vain did he enter into alliance with Sabako of Egypt,
who encouraged him to withhold his annual tribute
from Pul's successor, Shalmaneser. The Assyrian de-
clared war, fought the decisive battle in the historic
plain of Esdraelon. Here was Hoshea taken, the "bow
of Israel" utterly broken. For three years more Shalmaneser besieged Samaria. Egypt, the ally, failed to ap-
pear; the city fell. Twenty-seven thousand two hundred
Samaritans went into captivity. The kingdom of Jeroboam was ended, after an existence of two hundred and
fifteen years.

How Hoshea died we know not. Perhaps in prison,
perhaps by execution, maybe by suicide. What matters
it? The kings of Israel are dead. Long live the kings!

*II Kings 17:1 ff.*

# Hezekiah

STATESMAN, POET, RELIGIOUS REFORMER, FIGHTER, EN-
gineer and antiquarian, Hezekiah is the most versatile
and valuable of Judah's kings. It was to him she owed
her temporary recovery, her ability to outlive Samaria
by nearly a century and a half.

He restored the damage done by his father, Ahaz. He
reopened the Temple doors, relighted the lamps, restored the old altars and worship. After sixteen days of
cleansing, the proud Levites stood before him to report,
"We have cleansed all the House of the Lord." In
cleansing the Temple of Judah, Hezekiah had cleansed
her heart. And in her heart lay her strength.

He overran Philistia and he was overrun by Sennacherib, held in his city "like a bird in a cage," and he
paid heavy tribute to the Assyrian before he got out!
Hardly had Sennacherib turned away, however, before
Hezekiah was girding his loins to fight him again. Sennacherib came back to meet defeat; he never fought
Judah again.

You were great and you were godly, Hezekiah. You
did the impossible in an impossible hour, with an impossible people. But you came too late in the day. The
past and the future were too much for your present.

*II Kings 18:1-20:21; II Chronicles 29:1-32:33.*

# *Sennacherib*

PUL LIKED PUL. SENNACHERIB WORSHIPED SENNA-cherib. Born in the purple (his father was the great Sargon) and bred as crown prince, he grew up to be the acme of pride and the limit of arrogance. He describes himself as "the great king, the powerful king, the king of the Assyrians, of the nations, of the four regions, the diligent ruler, the favorite of the great gods, the observer of the sworn faith, the guardian of law, the establisher of monuments, the noble hero, the strong warrior, the first of kings, the punisher of unbelievers, the destroyer of wicked men!"

Pride or no pride, he was a most energetic soldier, and one of the ablest administrators ever to command the resources of a vast empire. He recovered Babylonia; he fought Phœnicia under Elulaeus, Judah under Hezekiah, Philistia under Zidqua, Egypt under Tirhakah. He led a countless multitude in chains. He created Nineveh as a metropolis of his empire and built its great wall; he built also the great palace of Kouyunjik, which alone was triumph enough for any man.

Conquests and palaces were the breath of his life. Had he died naturally, he would have died sighing for more worlds to conquer.

*II Chronicles 32:1 ff.; Isaiah 36:1-37.*

# *Manasseh*

At twelve, Manasseh the Mad was on the throne, a boy at the mercy of a group of court nobles who hated the Mosaic Code and loved the levity and laxity of Baal. They made him over into a fanatical persecutor of the worshipers of Jehovah. He negated every good act of his father. He took Baalism actually into the Temple, restored high-place worship, sacrificed his own child to Moloch and encouraged others to sacrifice theirs, offered incense to the sun, the moon, and to the twelve signs of the zodiac. He persecuted the prophets; he killed old Isaiah.

He rebelled against Ashurbanipal (Sennacherib's grandson) and refused to pay tribute. The Assyrians smashed his armies and led him by a ring through his lips to prison in Babylon. Released and allowed to reign again, he repented. He swept away the old gods and idols and tried to lead the nation back to Jehovah. It was an idle gesture. Repentance now could not correct the chaos of the early years. The people loathed him. He was still Manasseh the Mad, unclean, unworthy, unwanted.

*II Kings 21:1 ff.; II Chronicles 33:1 ff.*

# *Moloch*

To know a people, one must know their gods. To know Manasseh the Mad and his people, one must know Moloch, to whom he sacrificed his son.

Moloch was the god of consuming fire, the burning sun-deity who smote the land with unfruitfulness and pestilence, who dried up springs and put poison in the wind. To appease his anger, incense, animals and children were sacrificed to him. Moloch had a penchant for children.

All over the land were his statues, a human figure with a bull's head and sloping, outstretched arms. Within his brass belly a great fire roared; mothers came with their children and babies and rolled them down the arms into the fiery furnace, pressing kisses to their lips when they cried out; screams were drowned by a din of flutes and kettle-drums. Mothers were forbidden to sob; if they wept, the sacrifice was without honor or reward.

Is it any wonder that a God of love had such a bitter fight to establish Himself against such a background?

*II Kings 21:6; II Chronicles 33:6.*

# Josiah

JOSIAH WAS EIGHT WHEN THEY MADE HIM KING. UNLIKE Manasseh, he never succumbed to the demoralizers; here was Hezekiah reborn, the most blameless of the kings. His reign was the sunset, the last ray of light before the coming night.

He revived true religion in all its purity; he swept idolaters and idols before him like leaves before a wind. His zeal increased when his high priest discovered the lost Book of the Law; he read it aloud to the people, end to end, and followed the reading with a great national reformation. The faithful caught their second wind. If only the race had not been so far run!

The rest of Josiah's reign is darkness. He tried to contest the passage of the troops of Necho of Egypt across his soil (Belgium *vs.* Germany!), and in the battle at Megiddo he perished. Great was the lamentation of Judah over her godliest king; it endured for generations.

He did the work of ten men. One man destroyed it: Nebuchadnezzar!

*II Kings 22:1-23:30; II Chronicles 34:1-35:27.*

# *Jehoiakim*

JEHOAHAZ FOLLOWED JOSIAH. WITHIN THREE MONTHS
Necho (he whom Josiah had defied) took him in chains
to Egypt. Necho had been prospering; he was master
now of all between Samaria and the Euphrates. He was
king-maker, king-breaker, too. He cared not that Judah,
in ninety short days, had learned to love Jehoahaz; it
mattered not that Jeremiah bade them "weep sore for
him that goeth away," that this was to be the first Jewish prince to die in exile. Necho wanted a man of his
own on that throne; he wanted Jehoiakim.

Jehoiakim behaved himself for three years. He beau-
tified a few palaces and reared a host of heathen idols;
he cut to pieces with a penknife the roll of Jeremiah's
prophetic warnings and threw them into the fire. Then
he found himself caught between two other fires. The
Egyptian wolf had been devoured by the wolf from Babylon; Nebuchadnezzar whipped Necho; Judah changed
masters. Jehoiakim rebelled against the new wolf; he
was cornered and killed.

A natural product of Oriental monarchy, and the last
of them! The last of the blind, cruel, luxurious, dis-
graceful princes of the house of David.

*II Kings 22:31-24:7; II Chronicles 36:1 ff.;*
*Jeremiah 22:10; 36:20 ff.*

146

# Jehoiachin

NEBUCHADNEZZAR WAS MOST CONSIDERATE. JEHOIAKIM the rebel was dead, but the Babylonian graciously allowed the heir apparent, Jehoiachin, to mount the throne of his father. Considerate? Clever! Jehoiachin was just the man to keep the morale of the vassal state at lowest ebb. He did much evil in the sight of the Lord, provoking Jeremiah to call him "a despised vessel, a vessel wherein none delighteth." Nebuchadnezzar, watching him closely, soon became suspicious of him, marched on Jerusalem, took it, looted the Temple, seized the king, the court, and the able-bodied men of the city.

For thirty-seven years Jehoiachin languished in a dungeon. Hope left him; when he heard that Nebuchadnezzar was dead, he *knew* the world would forget him in his dark hole. What then was his amazement when Evilmerodach, the new king, brought him up out of his cell, gave him silks, a scepter and a salary, made him first of Babylon's captive kings! He ate daily with the royal family.

Why, no one but Evilmerodach shall ever know.

*II Kings 24:8 ff.; 25:27 ff.; II Chronicles 36:9 ff.;
Jeremiah 22:28.*

# Zedekiah

WHILE JEHOIACHIN FELL AND ROSE IN BABYLON, HIS brother Zedekiah (born Mattaniah) rose and fell in Judah. Judah fell with him, never to rise again. It was the end.

More weak than wicked, Zedekiah began as friend of justice and the Law, ended by walking in the ruts of evil left by his fathers. He began as Nebuchadnezzar's obedient servant; he ended in Nebuchadnezzar's jail.

He made a secret treaty with Hophra of Egypt, who promised to help him throw off the Assyrian yoke. Hophra deceived him. When Nebuchadnezzar marched to put down the rebellion of Zedekiah, Hophra failed to help. Jerusalem was besieged. For eighteen months she was besieged. Food ran out. Living skeletons defended the walls. Rich ladies in rich crimson gowns clawed the dunghills for food. Children dropped in the streets; fond parents ate their babies. Eighteen months! Then the besiegers found a breach in the wall, swept through it, and the sack began. No horror was spared. The gutters ran red, the city was on fire. Zedekiah himself was taken, his sons were killed before his eyes, and his eyes torn out. In fetters he went to Babylon. There he died.

*Fini la guerre. Fini, Judah!*

*II Kings 24:17-25:21; II Chronicles 36:11 ff.*

# *Nebuchadnezzar*

ALL ROADS LED TO BABYLON WHILE NEBUCHADNEZZAR ruled; broad, level, ribbon-like roads crowded with marching captives from Egypt, Judah, Syria; roads flanked by obelisks, monuments, palaces, temples, gardens, winding up to a dream city built on the site of old Babel's tower; a reborn city of a thousand flowered terraces and temple towers, shining in marble and silver like the stars of heaven. The "hanging" gardens, seventh wonder of the world, were there. Nebuchadnezzar! Builder of empires, terraces, temples.

In all these things he was very religious; his inscriptions have the spiritual fervor of Old Testament poetry. He loved the god Marduk. Daniel, Jewish prophet and Babylonian captive, hated Marduk. Therefore Daniel painted the black side of Nebuchadnezzar's character.

He had a black side. He put three Hebrew boys in a furnace; he cursed and he killed and he oppressed and he built for himself a tower of vanity from which he fell to the estate of a beast, eating grass. He was cruel with the people and fickle with the gods. But (think on this thing!) he cried once in deep sincerity, "Blessed be the God of Shadrach, Meshach, and Abed-nego."

*Daniel 2:36 ff.; 31:13 ff., 28.*

149

# *Shadrach*

THE JEWS OF THE CAPTIVITY (POOR NAME FOR IT) were of two species, the wailers and the passive resisters. "By the rivers of Babylon we sat down and wept": that was the swan-song of the mournful majority. Some few refused to wail, to worship Babylon's idols, to eat unclean food, or to stop praying to Israel's God. Shadrach refused.

Shadrach, Meshach, and Abed-nego! Heroes may come and heroes may go, but . . . Nebuchadnezzar cast them into his fiery furnace for refusing to worship his golden image. Nebuchadnezzar rubbed his eyes as they walked the red coals. A fourth ("like the Son of God") walked with them. They came out unsinged, unscorched, still passive resisters. "Yea, though I walk through the valley of the shadow of death . . ."

Their miraculous delivery from death absorbs us. Their constancy in life should stir us. Before they entered the flames they vowed: "If not [if our God fails to save us,] we will not serve *thy* gods . . ." They never expected to come out alive!

There is powerful symbolism here. In the fires of the Captivity Israel's faith was being tried. The Hebrew state was flowing, molten, into Judaism.

*Psalm 137:1; Daniel 3:13 ff.*

# *Belshazzar*

HISTORICALLY, BELSHAZZAR IS HARD TO PLACE. CON-
temporary records have no Babylonian king of this
name. But morally, may he live forever! He is indispensable to an understanding of Babylon and Babylon's
fall.

He set a great feast for his harem and his lords, a
maudlin bacchanalia in which they drank from golden
goblets pilfered from the Temple of Jerusalem. At the
height of the carousal, a phantom hand appeared, writing a warning on the wall: "Mene, Mene, Tekel, Uphar-
sin." None of the Chaldean wise men could tell Belshazzar what it meant. Daniel told him: he had been
weighed and found wanting; his kingdom was about to
pass to the Medes and the Persians. That day Daniel
was honored; that night Belshazzar was slain; that year
Cyrus the Persian took Babylon.

Belshazzar's historicity is of little moment. Here is a
good picture of Babylon in the days of the Captivity;
here is a fine tribute to the courage and intelligence of
the Captivity Jew; here is a pertinent study of the causes
of empire collapse. Long power begets carelessness;
carelessness begets impiety; impiety begets immorality;
immorality begets deterioration and collapse.

*Daniel 5:1 ff.*

# Darius

"AND DARIUS THE MEDIAN TOOK THE KINGDOM." MORE historical confusion! No Darius preceded Persian Cyrus. Perhaps the chronicler had reference to Gobryas, who received the kingdom for Cyrus; perhaps he meant Darius Hystaspes, father of Xerxes (Ahasuerus). His identity is lost; his Biblical fame rests on one act—he sent Daniel to the lion's den.

And while he may be the victim of many a historical "perhaps," there is no "perhaps" about his people. The Medes lived east of Assyria; they were subdued by Assyria; they joined with the Babylonians to destroy Nineveh, with the Persians to destroy Babylon. In the days of "Darius the Mede" this empire of Medo-Persia absorbed all Median, Assyrian, and Chaldean Jews. Absorbed them and lost them. Ten tribes of Israel disappeared as completely as though the earth had yawned and swallowed them up. We are searching for them yet. They are still the Ten Lost Tribes.

Media had a finer son than Darius. Zoroaster lived and taught there in the seventh century B.C. Zoroaster and Jesus had much in common. We have an electric-light bulb named for Zoroaster's god—Mazda, meaning "light."

# Cyrus

HIS GRANDFATHER ORDERED HIM KILLED AT BIRTH. A shepherd saved him. A good shepherd. He saved Cyrus the Great, founder of the great Persian Empire and liberator of a great people.

His drive and genius placed him soon at the head of the Persians. Within ten years he had overcome King Crœsus of Lydia, King Amasis of Egypt, King Nabonidus of Babylon; he was master of the greatest empire the world had yet seen, chief ruler of all Asia.

He said to the Jews in Babylon, "Go home now." After sixty years . . . go home! That made him their friend. He said to them, also, "Rebuild your Temple." That made him friend of God. Isaiah calls him the "anointed," the chosen instrument of the divine judgment on Babylon.

His kingdom passed in time to the Greeks; the Greeks bowed to the Romans. A battle here, a battle there, then rust and dust and new masters. The real achievement of Cyrus was no battle, no war, no conquest. It was his edict for the rebuilding of the Temple. That was the genesis of Judaism. It meant that a nation had become a church.

*II Chronicles 36:22 f.; Isaiah 45:1.*

# *Zerubbabel*

THOSE WHO LOVED GOD WENT HOME FIRST. CYRUS THE Generous gave them back the sacred treasures of their Temple; their fellow captives gave them gold, goods, and beasts. They marched out jubilant, singing, forty thousand strong. At their head marched Sheshbazzar, custodian of their treasures and first Restoration governor, and Zerubbabel, second governor, Temple-builder, and (says Zechariah) their coming Messiah.

At the Feast of Tabernacles, on the anniversary of the dedication of Solomon's Temple, they placed the new altar. Later the Temple foundations were laid with a great choir singing, the young men cheering and the elders weeping.

There was less cheering as Zerubbabel proceeded with the building. Opposition was everywhere; the Samaritans, the Jews, his enemies, did all in their power to stop it. Once it did stop. For sixteen years the ring of the hammer and the song of the saw were not heard. But Zerubbabel (plus Zechariah and Haggai) saw it through. In the sixth year of Darius it was finished.

He was a governor neither long nor successful. His forte was temple-building. A vital forte for any man. No religion can exist without temples.

*Ezra 1:1 ff.; 3:1 ff.; 4:1 ff.; 6:15;*
*Zechariah 3:8; 4:6 ff.*

# Nehemiah

GREAT CRISES MAKE GREAT MEN. THE CRISIS OF THE Restoration produced Nehemiah. Mark him well, all ye who worship heroes. Mark him as he weeps in midnight vigil over fallen Jerusalem; mark him as he rages, spear in one hand, trowel in the other, in Herculean fury to rebuild the city wall, a dynamo of action, a man of prayer and an engineer. In fifty-two days the wall is done, the gates are hung, and Nehemiah is gone back to Babylon!

Returning, he found an Augean stable to be cleaned. The Sabbath was being desecrated; the priests and Levites were without support; mixed marriages were popular. The holy Hercules goes into action again. He is vehement, tireless, determined. Of one culprit-husband he says, "I chased him from me!" Others he cursed, or smote, or pulled out their hair.

Nehemiah did for politics what Ezra later did for religion. He was more emotional and patriotic, therefore more beloved than Ezra. He had the irresistible combination of cool brain and hot heart. He gave unsparingly of both for the happiness of his people and the preservation of their faith. Can mortal man do more?

*Nehemiah 1:4 ff.; 4:6, 15 ff.; 6:15; 13:6 ff.; 28.*

# *Ezra*

BACK IN BABYLON, EZRA FUMED. THE APOSTASY AND timidity of the Jerusalem colony sickened his heart and stirred his hand. He mobilized fifteen hundred men, loaded a caravan with bread, silver, and gold, and started for . . . home. It was a four months' trek across the desert, as exciting as the trek of the Mormon wagon-train or the Klondike mushers of '96.

Ezra lost no time when he reached Jerusalem; he was master of the city from the moment he arrived. He enforced separation on all men who had married foreign wives; that was social reform. He unpacked from the caravan a roll of the Law (that great body of religious practice and order which forms the bulk of our Pentateuch) and instructed the people in it. That was religious reform. He made their souls come alive with love of the Law; he gave them, through it, an inner fire which has been their protection ever since, which they have carried as wandering Jews, Prometheus-like, down to the ends of the earth. He gave them Judaism and the Priestly Code. Then he vanished. Tradition has him buried in Persia.

*Ezra 7:1-10:16; Nehemiah 8:1 ff.*

# *Ahasuerus*

To the Biblical historian he is Ahasuerus, king of Persia while the Jews were there; to the secular writer he is Xerxes I, the sottish, babyish son of Darius who thought to conquer Athens and the Greeks. He was not the man for that. He had never conquered himself.

He spent four years preparing to avenge the defeat of his father by the Greeks at Marathon. He built a fleet of twelve hundred battleships; he threw a bridge of boats across the Hellespont and took over it an army which Herodotus says was two million strong. (A storm destroyed his first birdge; Xerxes, in imbecilic rage, scourged the waters with three hundred lashes!) The Spartans almost stopped him at Thermopylæ; the Athenians, at Salamis, destroyed his fleet and sent him running back across his bridge of boats. It was the Persians' largest army, their greatest battle and most significant defeat. It turned civilization's tide.

At home, at court, he was a jackdaw in peacock's feathers. Drunk, he insulted a noble queen and lost her; Haman tricked him; Esther swayed him; he was a reed bowing to every wind that blew.

*Ezra 4:6; Esther 1:10 ff.; 3:8 ff.; 5:1 ff.*

# Vashti

Vashti for pride
Was set aside,

SAID THE OLD NEW ENGLAND READER. THE READER WAS wrong. Queen Vashti was set aside by a drunken husband who did not know what he was doing, and who regretted it when he sobered up.

Ahasuerus was on a seven-day spree with the princes and nobles of his court. Inebriated to the point of lust, he demanded of his beautiful queen that she parade herself, her charms, her beauty, before his loutish courtiers. Vashti rebelled. She said, "No." Ahasuerus, in the high flush of intoxication and on the advice of his comrades, deposed her.

For pride? Given more Vashtis, the world would have fewer drunkards. When she chose deposition rather than dishonor, she took first honors for her sex; when she put off the diadem of Persia she put on a crown which lay beyond the power of Ahasuerus to give or take away: the crown of exalted womanhood.

Four years later a Jewish girl named Esther took her place in the palace of Shushan.

*Esther 1:10 ff.; 2:16 ff.*

# *Memucan*

"WHAT SHALL WE DO UNTO THE QUEEN VASHTI, according to law . . . ?" asked Ahasuerus of his besotted nobles. Memucan told him what to do. Memucan was a gem. So was his suggestion.

He was terribly frightened at the insubordination of Vashti. She had done wrong, he felt, to "all the people." Especially, to the husbands. Why, think of it! if this thing were allowed to pass unrebuked, *all* the ladies would be trying it. A most dangerous precedent, O king! They shall despise their husbands! Let Vashti be deposed, and soon. And let a law be passed that "every man shall rule in his own house." The alcoholic parliament of worried husbands agreed unanimously: it must be done. It was done.

Respect for husbands by due process of law! Legislated love! The Bible does not tell us how it all worked out; likely, it did not work at all. Some husbands in Shushan probably never mentioned it to their wives.

A happy marriage relation depends upon something else than statute-books; love and respect are won and never commanded. That is as true for husbands as for wives.

*Esther 1:15 ff.*

# *Mordecai*

With Vashti divorced, Ahasuerus sought a new queen. He found one in the person of Esther, in the house of Jewish Mordecai, her cousin.

Mordecai was shrewd. His skillful coaching of the young Esther saved his people from destruction; his timely warning to the king brought him into the royal favor. Mordecai was proud. He refused to pay homage, to bow his head to Haman (Prime Minister, attention-lover). Haman vowed to kill him for that. He even built the gallows for the Jew. Thanks to Esther, Mordecai never swung.

Rebuked by the courtiers for his pride, Mordecai replied, stiffly, "I am a Jew." There is the essence of the Book of Esther. There is no religious conviction or zeal in these Esther-characters; the name of God is mentioned nowhere in the Book. Their religion is a narrow, unethical nationalism; their creed is "Love your own, hate your enemies."

Saved by Esther from the gallows, Mordecai lived long and well, clad in garments of pure linen and purple, a gold crown on his head. But Persian garments could never make a Persian of Mordecai. . . . "I am a Jew."

*Esther 2:7; 2:21 ff.; 3:2 ff.; 5:14; 6:10 ff.*

# *Haman*

HAMAN WAS NOT PERSIAN. HE WAS AN AMALEKITE. Which explains a great deal. When Mordecai refused to bow to him, the traditional, undying hatred of Amalekite for Jew burst into flame. He would destroy not only Mordecai, but every Jew in Persia! With the king's consent, a decree was published. On the thirteenth day of the month Adar (March) the foreigners were to die.

Mordecai rent his clothes when he heard of it; the Jews mourned, fasted, and wept; Esther gave two dinner parties. Her guests were Haman and the king. Haman was elated. Invited by the queen!

At the first banquet Esther lost her nerve . . . and invited the guests back for another. In the interlude between them Haman was mortified, sent by Ahasuerus to heap royal honors on Mordecai, who, the king had just learned, had once saved his life.

At the second banquet Esther did it. She denounced Haman before the king, exposing his plot against her people. By nightfall Haman was swinging on the gallows he had prepared for Mordecai.

There was no public funeral. Nobody liked Haman . . . except Haman.

*Esther 3:1 ff.; 13, 15; 5:7 ff.; 6:10 ff.; 7:6 ff.*

# *Zeresh*

THERE ARE TWO WIVES' TALES IN THE BOOK OF ESTHER. One is the tale of Vashti, who was too good for her husband; the other, the tale of Zeresh, the wife of Haman, who flattered her husband's self-conceit and hastened his destruction.

Haman came home with his invitation to Esther's banquet, delirious with joy. Zeresh became delirious with him. Now he was getting somewhere, this rich husband of hers! Her social position was bound to improve as he grew in power, in favor with the royal family.

She noticed that he was still irked over that stubborn Mordecai. She advised him. Build a gallows for Mordecai, fifty cubits high; let him be swinging in the wind while you are feasting in the palace! ". . . go thou in merrily with the king unto the banquet."

When the tide turned and Haman saw that he was lost, he turned to her for help. He met only tears and wailing. Zeresh had nothing for a crisis.

The fifty-cubit gallows was as much hers as Haman's.

*Esther 5:14; 6:13.*

162

# Esther

ESTHER HAD A BLUE-BLOOD GENEALOGY. SHE WAS COUS-
in and foster-daughter to Mordecai, a Benjamite descendant of Kish, the father of Saul. Oddly enough,
both Esther and Mordecai were named for Babylonian
gods—Ishtar and Marduk.

She had courage. She went in alone, unsummoned,
unannounced, to plead for her people before a capricious king. Luckily, she found him in good humor. But
she had counted the cost of finding him ill-humored.
Her "if I perish, I perish," is the epitome of altruism;
her impassioned plea for her life and the lives of her
people is an epic of devotional heroism.

Esther had a streak of vengefulness. She took an unfair advantage of Haman when he groveled at her feet,
seeking mercy. She aided in the slaughter of her people's enemies when the tables were turned in their favor.
She asked for the hanging of Haman's sons.

But Esther's faults are outweighed by Esther's self-
denial. She was as virtuous as she was fair, dutiful to
both her foster-father and her king, loyal to her people
and her God. She offered to lay down her life for her
friends. Greater love hath no man than this . . .

*Esther 2:5 ff.; 4:16; 5:1 ff.; 7:3 ff.; 9:13.*

# *Job*

JOB LIVED IN UZ. HE WAS PERFECT. RIGHTEOUS. GOD-
fearing. He had seven sons, three daughters, sheep,
camels, mules by the thousand. God and Satan fought
for Job's soul, as they fight for yours and mine. Job suffered, horribly, as they fought.

Thieves stole and lightning killed his flocks. A hurri-
cane blew down his house and killed his seven sons.
"The Lord gave, and the Lord hath taken away," said
Job. His soul was worth fighting for.

He was smitten with boils from head to foot; his wife
mocked his faith, told him to curse God and die. He rebuked her. But when three friends came to "comfort"
him and remained to condemn him, Job broke, and
cursed the day he was born.

Job's friends wounded his heart; they could not
break it. He came back to faith. He accepted his suffering as a test of his faith. He cannot understand it, nor
God. Yet he accepts both. He holds fast. Satan is defeated, God triumphs. The friends are confounded.
Job's prosperity and happiness are restored.

Job left us certain eternally unanswered questions:
Why must the righteous suffer! What is the purpose of
suffering? What is God like?

● *Job 1:1 ff.; 2:7 ff.; 3:1; 42:1 ff.*

# *Eliphaz*

ELIPHAZ WAS THE OLDEST OF THE THREE "FRIENDS" OF Job. He was pompous. Too pompous. He was certain he knew God's ways and purposes. Too certain. He had three arguments. Three too many.

No man was perfect, he said, until he had the chastisement of suffering. Suffering was the penalty of previous sin. You have sinned, Job. Accept this suffering. You shall be better for it. Job insisted that he had *not* sinned. Prove it, Eliphaz. Eliphaz changed the subject.

"Should a man utter vain knowledge . . . ?"

"You are proud, Job. You shall be rebuked. It is foolish and wicked to ask God questions or to challenge His ways." It was here that Job's patience cracked. He, proud? "Miserable comforters are ye all."

Eliphaz tried again. "Look back, Job," he says in effect, "and you will surely find an old, forgotten sin somewhere." Job recalled no sin.

Eliphaz was a stickler for his particular theological theory. Some theologians think more of their theories than they do of the truth. That in itself is sin! Eliphaz could only talk about God. No man ever found God by talking about Him. What Eliphaz needed was to suffer a little.

*Job 5:17; 15:1; 16:2; 22:2 ff.*

# *Bildad*

BILDAD WAS CONSERVATIVE AND VAGUE. HE WAS THE traditionalist of the group. He referred boil-smitten Job to antiquity for comfort.

Read history, said Bildad! See how the righteous always prosper there! How the wicked always suffer! (Where did you study your history, Bildad?) Take courage, Job; if you are really righteous, God will make things right.

He rebuked Job for losing patience with the friends. Listen to us, man. We have wisdom! He scored the wicked roundly, predicting divers punishments and doom. (Did Dante study Bildad before he wrote his *Hell?*) He made Job mad: "How long will ye vex my soul, and break me in pieces with words?" I am suffering, and you sit here talking.

That silenced Bildad. He made a feeble remark to the effect that men should never attempt to justify themselves, and . . . forever after held his peace.

Eliphaz, at least, had brought out the majesty of God. Bildad had only appealed to history (ignorantly, at that) while it was the present—and the future—that worried Job.

Said Will Shakespeare: "Words, words, mere words, no matter from the heart."

*Job 8:8 ff.; 18:2; 19:2; 25:4.*

# Zophar

ZOPHAR, THE YOUNGEST OF THE TRIO, IS A PUZZLE. SOME say he was rough and noisy; others thinks he was a philosopher, of the agnostic school.

His speech flowed hot, like lava from the lip of Vesuvius; his tongue was quicker than his brain. He lectured Job (an old man) severely for his "self-righteousness." Repent, Job. God may yet save you. Stop trying to understand God. Who by searching may find Him? Humble yourself. Pour dust on your head.

Job waxed sarcastic over this explosion: "No doubt ye are the people, and wisdom shall die with you." Then he said, evenly, "I am not inferior to you."

That should have silenced Zophar; it didn't. He was too young, too talkative. He rambled on. He said nothing. He repeated what he had said before. He aped Bildad about the punishment of the wicked. He told Job to be careful. Then he said no more. Perhaps the conversation was too deep for him to follow.

Eliphaz had a theory, and he worked it hard; Bildad had words, and he piled them up; Zophar had nothing, and he used it well. Nurses in hospitals say that "visiting hours" often have a bad effect on patients' health.

*Job 11:7 ff.; 12:2 f.; 20:12 ff.*

# *Elihu*

ELIHU HAD "I" TROUBLE. ANGRY AT JOB FOR HIS COM-
plaining and at the three friends for their failure, he bade
them all keep still: "I will speak, that *I* may be re-
freshed. . . . *I* will open *my* lips . . . hold thy lips, and *I*
will teach thee wisdom." The flood that poured from his
lips was so bombastic, conceited, ludicrous, that poor
Job, weary and astounded, refused even to attempt an
answer.

Elihu had two good arguments. One was that God
sends "visions and suffering" to help men; God's justice
is perfect; men should not dispute it; all man can do is
to practice goodness and faith; God will reward that.
The other was that no man can ever know anything
about God. God is beyond us.

First, he talks like a man on very, very intimate terms
with God. Then he says that God is incomprehensible!

So the arguments end, about where they started. God
spoke directly to Job in a whirlwind, and (for Job) the
argument was settled. But the four visitors did more
harm than they did good. They should have brought
some bandages for the sores, some ointment for the
boils.

*Job 32:20 ff.; 33:14 ff.; 36:26; 38:1 ff.*

# Amos

A DULL RUMBLE OF THUNDER ROLLED OUT OF THE DES-
ert of Tekoa. Out of the desert, in the voice of a man.
Bearded, brawned, afire, Amos was God's thunder over
Israel, the thunder prelude to the gathering storm, the
first fighting picket of a new battalia of prophets.

His eyes and lips threw flame. The rich blanched as
he excoriated them for "selling the righteous for silver,
the poor for a pair of shoes," for filling their hewn-
stone houses with the spoil of robbery! Hypocrites were
in a funk before their altars as he shouted, "I hate, I despise your feasts." The soul of religion had fled; it was
divorced from morality. The outside of the cup was pol-
ished gold, the inside tarnished and foul.

Stop, O Israel! God wants no more of your two-faced
sacrifice. God, all-righteous himself, *demands* righteousness. Righteousness, righteousness, righteousness! "Let
judgment [justice] roll down as waters, and righteousness as a mighty stream." Jehovah is the God of the
whole earth (a new note), but He loves Israel best.
Therefore He expects more of Israel. Privilege brings
responsibility.

Repent, O Israel. There was no repentance. Amos
died. So did Israel.

*Amos 2:6; 3:2; 5:21, 24; 8:10 ff.*

# Hosea

AMOS, THE THUNDERER, PROPHET OF WRATH, GAVE WAY to Hosea, prophet of love. Amos addressed the conscience, Hosea the heart. One was the soul of fury, the other the essence of tenderness.

The truth came to Amos in the desert solitudes; it met Hosea on his own doorstep. He married a girl at God's command, wooed her, loved her, lost her. Gomer left him to play the harlot in the street. In Hosea's anguished soul a clean light flashed; he saw it! What Gomer was to him, Israel was to God. The love covenant of wilderness days had been violated as Israel played the harlot with her Baals. He must tell Israel.

He told Israel . . . in the saddest language prophet ever spoke. As wrathful as Amos in denouncing the sins and idolatries of his hour, he stood on higher ground when he pictured God as waiting, as he had waited for Gomer, to come home. Then he added consolation to condemnation and complaint. If you would understand the Gospel of Jesus, his view of God, his love of mankind, read Hosea.

Love . . . beareth all things . . . hopeth . . . endureth all things. God and Hosea . . . loving . . . forgiving . . . waiting.

*Hosea 1:2 ff.; 4:11 ff.; 6:4 ff.; 4:8 ff.*

# Isaiah

IN THE MIGHTY CONSTELLATION OF THE PROPHETS Isaiah is mightiest. He puts all others in eclipse. His least word fell like the blow of a battle-axe; he spoke in poetry, so eloquent that it is lost among the stars.

Young, he had a vision and heard a call; he was to warn Judah of the judgment to come; the Assyrian wolf (the weapon of judgment) growls in all his preaching. As statesman, he fought bitterly the kings who left Jehovah to put their trust in foreign alliance. As preacher he strove to call the people back from their blasphemous sacrifices to genuine justice and humanity. God was bored with their hollow prayers. He demanded holiness. Holiness, holiness, holiness. King and commoner laughed at that.

Despairing of them, Isaiah faced the future. Some would survive the Assyrian scourge, he said. A *righteous remnant* would survive, to rear a new house of faith and holiness on today's dead ashes. Remnant, remnant, remnant! Over them would come to rule a Messiah, who would be called Wonderful, Counselor, The Mighty God, The Everlasting Father, The Prince of Peace.

Isaiah promised it. Jesus fulfilled it.

*Isaiah 1:10 ff.; 6:1 ff.; 7:3 ff.; 6:6; 10:21 ff.*

# *Micah*

POLES APART FROM ISAIAH WAS HIS CONTEMPORARY,
Micah. Isaiah was cultured and refined; Micah was a
peasant, a man of the people, the champion and the
tribune of the poor.

He stepped forth, alone, from the ranks of the oppressed to denounce the oppressor. He mourned the
lack of justice for the poor. Justice, justice, justice. He
flayed the rich who "flayed the poor and ate their flesh,"
who built their houses of iniquity and blood. He
scorned the professional prophets; they were liars, wine-
bibbers.

National calamity was sure to come, said Micah.
"Therefore shall Zion . . . be plowed as a field, and
Jerusalem shall become heaps . . ." But after that, the
Messiah would come. Come, from Bethlehem.

Twice he reached real heights. Once he talked of the
nations beating their swords into plowshares, their
spears into pruning-hooks. (Suppose we had tried that
in 1914?) Again, he asked, ". . . what doth the Lord re-
quire of thee, but to do justly, and to love mercy, and to
walk humbly with thy God?" A good prescription for
our day of spiritual confusion, when we preach with
Christly passion for social justice and reform!

*Micah 3:1 ff.; 4:3; 5:2 ff.; 6:8.*

# *Nahum*

NAHUM IS A THROWBACK FROM THE PEAKS OF PROPHECY
reached by Amos and Isaiah to the dark valleys of bar-
barism. He had the tongue of a poet, the mind of a patriot, the heart of a Cain. His Book is one long mad ex-
ultation over the impending destruction of Nineveh.

Nowhere does he speak of the reforms of Josiah or
the influence of Jeremiah, so important in his day.
Wearing the blinders of a narrow patriotic passion, he
could see nothing but burning Nineveh. On every side
were things he should have seen. But an enemy of
Judah was perishing; a robber people, they were at last
in chains. The vengeance of God was on Assyria. Vengeance, vengeance, vengeance. Exult, O Judah, your old
enemy is dead!

Nahum grasped one truth with fierce intensity. God
*does* punish violence, *does* vindicate the righteous and
punish the oppressors. But he neglected to apply that
truth to his own people, as other prophets had done.
His vision was only outward; theirs, outward and inward.

He seems to be as much misplaced among the prophets as Mars would be at a peace conference.

*Nahum 1:2; 3:1 ff.*

# Zephaniah

ZEPHANIAH WAS THE PROPHET OF TERROR AND DOOM, the perfect pessimist. He had none of Nahum's vengeful joy; nor had he Nahum's blinders. But he did what Nahum had left undone. He saw not only Nineveh, but Judah and Jerusalem and all the nations of the earth, going down together in the Judgment Day, the Last Day, the Great Day of Jehovah, to be judged by a great and just Jehovah who held all nations in the hollow of His hand. The Day, the Day, the Day! Punishment was certain. False worshipers, waverers, and apostates had knit well the threads of doom on a loom of evil destiny; princes who were roaring lions, judges who were ravening wolves, prophets who were light and treacherous persons had cast the die. "I will utterly consume *all* things from off the land, saith the Lord." The Second Deluge?

Zephaniah, like Isaiah, has a righteous remnant to be rescued. God is not only just, but merciful. The thunderclouds of divine wrath are followed by the sunshine of divine forgiveness. God is ruler of all nations, peoples, races, demanding righteousness of all. That is Zephaniah's preaching. That is the golden cord on which the finest pearls of Hebrew prophecy are strung. That is the "ethical monotheism of the prophets."

*Zephaniah 1:2, 7 ff.; 3:1 ff.; 13 ff.*

# *Habakkuk*

HABAKKUK WAS PROPHECY'S THOMAS, AN HONEST, OPEN seeker after God. He saw "truth forever on the scaffold, wrong forever on the throne," and he asked God why. He saw through a glass, darkly, until he climbed a high tower (of faith) to talk with God. Then he saw face to face.

Habakkuk saw Ninevah fall to Babylon, saw the Chaldean become a crueler tyrant over Judah than the Assyrian. How could God do this? How could such barbarians do His will? So Godless a people be his instrument?

Back came the answer: Be patient, Habakkuk. The Chaldean *is* mine instrument, but he shall destroy himself, and the righteous in Judah shall be saved by faith. Faith, faith, faith! God moves mysteriously . . . but He moves. Patience. Faith.

Habakkuk descends his tower, no longer prophet of doubt, but prophet of faith. He knows, now. "The Lord is in his holy temple. . . ." God's in his heaven, all's right with the world. . . . He knows that "the earth shall be filled with the knowledge of the glory of the Lord, as the waters cover the sea."

Honest questioners usually find an honest God.

*Habakkuk 1:5 ff.; 2:1 ff.; 14, 20.*

# *Obadiah*

OBADIAH, THE PROPHET, WEPT IN BABYLON, BUT HE wept not tears of despair. He was bitter. He shook his fist toward the horizon, toward Edom, and sang a hymn of hate to the Edomites. How he hated them! He had reason to. From the day the sons of Jacob had entered Canaan they had been in trouble with the sons of Esau. Saul, David, Solomon, Jehoram, and Amaziah had fought them; Amos, Jeremiah, and Ezekiel had cursed them. And while the Babylonians sacked Jerusalem, Edomites lined the hills around the city and shouted gleefully, "Down with it, down with it even unto the ground." Yes, Obadiah had reason. . . .

The coming vengence on the whole race is his single theme. He gloats over their fall, over Israel marching in to possess their land. His is anything but happy language, anything but spiritual. It is the long, deep cry of the embittered Jew against his age-old enemy. Obadiah was mad, and his anger, uncontrolled, made him the least of the twelve minor prophets.

Yet, the closing line of his book reveals a finer man. "The Kingdom shall be the Lord's," he says. That sounds quite like "Thy Kingdom come. . . ."

*Obadiah vv. 17, 21.*

# *Jeremiah*

HE BURIED HIS CLOTHES. HE DUG THEM UP. HE SAID TO Judah, "Your faith is like that. Once it was white and clean." But now . . . buried . . . moldy . . . a maggoty, ragged externalism instead of an inward fire. You drone vain words about "The Temple." Your Temple is a fetish, your faith magical farce. "Return, ye backsliding children. . . ." You may gain Jehovah's favor by change of life, by obedience to His moral law, but never by a fetish—Temple.

Dramatic, object-lesson-preacher Jeremiah! Prophet of the Inner Life! The highest, broadest, deepest of them all, as colorful as Joseph's cloak, as sad as Hosea, as brave as Jesus on the Cross. Jeremiah, the sad, majestic, melancholy man of God!

He was a minister sent to tell a sick man he must die. He saw sick Judah weaken, totter, fall. He saw Nabopolassar come, then Necho, and finally Nebuchadnezzar. All through the closing years he preached, prophesied, warned of the coming Exile, pleaded for a heart set right with God before the end. He saw his people scattered. Then he died.

He predicted a new Covenant, a day when God's law would be written on Jewish hearts instead of in Jewish books. He did not see it. Jesus did.

*Jeremiah 3:22; 7:4 ff.; 18:1 ff.; 19:1 ff.; 26:1 ff.;
31:31 ff.*

# *Baruch*

BARUCH WAS A PHENOMENON. IN AN AGE OF DISLOYALTY
he was loyal; in an hour of plunder, when he might have
sought "great things for himself" he chose to go down
to Egypt with Jeremiah. Born to wealth and the life of a
prince, he was content to be friend, amanuensis, and
Boswell to Jeremiah.

For twenty years he served the prophet. In the conflict with Jehoiakim he wrote the famous prophecy, read
it to the populace, received a hearing (through his influence) for it at the Court. When Jehoiakim destroyed
the roll, Baruch wrote another.

He was in prison for Jeremiah's sake when Jerusalem
fell; he was at his side among the Judeans left behind in
the Second Captivity; he went with him, under Johan-
an, to Egypt. There he stayed until the prophet died.
Tradition says he then went to Babylon, thence to join
Jeremiah again behind the inscrutable walls of the city
of death. Baruch probably welcomed death. What was
life without Jeremiah?

The Book of Jeremiah owes much to Baruch the sec-
retary; the personality of Jeremiah owes more to
Baruch the biographer. Thanks to him, the man from
Anathoth is the best known of the prophets.

*Jeremiah 36:1 ff.; 43:3, 6; 45:1 ff.*

# Ezekiel

AT MIDNIGHT HE COULD SEE. IN THE MIDST OF THE Captivity-wailing he heard the whir of angels' wings. Ezekiel was the prophet of the Exile, the chaplain marching with a nation condemned to the execution-place, the bridge of hope between Captivity and Restoration, the father of ecclesiastical Judaism and the evangelic forerunner of Jesus Christ the Lord.

He began as priest, as solid churchman, as ritualist to whom altar-ceremonial was meat and drink and all. But in Babylon, denied his altars and his great kneeling congregations, Ezekiel changed his message and his ways. The priest became a prophet; now he preached a God universal and transcendent, a new Messiah, a "Good Shepherd" leading his "flock." He talked of Israel's resurrection day, when God would gather together the nation's dry, dead bones, breathe life and spirit into them again. Above all else, he preached of *individual responsibility*. Nations, masses, no longer interested him. These were made up of individuals. Men, not nations, were the sinners. "The soul that sinneth, *it* shall die." Sin was personal, not collective.

A new God . . . a good shepherd . . . resurrection . . . personal responsibility. . . . Is this Ezekiel . . . or Jesus?

*Ezekiel 18:1 ff.; 34:11 ff.; 37:1 ff.*

179

# Daniel

WHOEVER PUT THOSE LIONS IN DANIEL'S BOOK? THEY are discordant; their roaring drowns the voice of the real prophet, their yawning jaws divert our eyes from the real man. The den is no place for Daniel; he soared higher than Ezekiel.

In courage he faced the beasts, in courage also turned his face from king to God in pagan Babylon. In wisdom he rose high at Nebuchadnezzar's Court, interpreting his dreams and visions, in wisdom also he lifted the hearts of Israel to honor the heroism of the past and plot the heroism of tomorrow. In faith he worshiped God in his own room, in faith kept preaching to all of the ultimate triumph of the Kingdom of God.

Ezekiel's Book is filled with whirring angels' wings; Daniel has their earthly footprints on every line and page. His are patron angels, talking, walking. Ezekiel has a dreamy, hazy resurrection; Daniel has a certain, practical one. Here, for the first time, is an Old Testament heaven, a resurrection for the wicked, an order of punishment and reward.

Daniel the Daring! He snatched hope from the lion-jaws of dissolution, sacred Utopia from the shadows of the Stygian shore.

*Daniel 2:17 ff.; 5:13 ff.; 6:10 ff.; 7:13 ff.; 12:2 f.*

# Haggai

THOSE WHO KNOW HIM FAINTLY CALL HIM QUAINT, THE odd one, the nonconformist of prophecy. He added this to prophecy: he called Zerubbabel the Messiah, which was wrong. He had none of Amos' thunder, Hosea's love, Isaiah's star-dust loftiness, or Ezekiel's whirring wings. Haggai was an exhorter, an enthusiast, a preacher with one idea who geared his preaching to his hour. "Build that Temple" was his message, the introduction, body, and conclusion of his preaching.

He saw one thing and saw it clearly: a religious community needed a common center of worship; the very existence of Jewish religion depended on the restoration of the Temple. When the returned exiles seemed too lazy to start, he whipped them into action with, "Build it, build it." When their spirits lagged, he exhorted them, "Build it, build it." When the Samaritans opposed, he overcame them with, "Build it, build it."

Say he was no prophet if you will. Criticize his motives, dub him externalist. But . . . church-builders must build ere preachers can preach. Some preachers use rhetoric, some use bricks. Neither can exist alone.

*Haggai 1:2 ff.; 2:4 ff.; 23.*

# Zechariah

ZECHARIAH WAS PROPHECY'S COLUMBUS, ITS DISCOV-erer, its visionary with his eye pinned to a blur on the sky-line. He has many visions (four horsemen, four horns, four workmen, a flying roll, and a golden candle-stick), and many angels (mediators); he speaks in terms of apocalyptic symbolism, hopeful, Messianic, *peacefully* triumphant. He discovered the devil and a young man with a measuring-line in his hand.

He named the devil Satan, made him a cunning tempter, an angel fallen. Look well as this Satan. He comes not out of the pits of wickedness, but out of the indifference of *good* men, in God's purposes gone wrong through human slothfulness.

And the boy with the measuring-line, laying out the lines of a new city wall! Said an angel, "Run, speak to this young man." . . . Tell him to build his Temple first, strengthen his soul before his gates; tell him that walls are futile . . . they shut one in, others out . . . that God wants expansion, not exclusion . . . that religion must roam and grow, not hibernate and die . . . that the im-pregnable fortresses of God are within the heart, not around the city. . . .

Run, speak to this young man!

*Zechariah 1:18 ff.; 2:4 ff.; 3:1 ff.; 4:2 ff.; 5:1 ff.; 6:1 ff.*

# *Joel*

THE BUZZ OF A LOCUST PLAGUE LED JOEL TO PROPHESY.
He watched them devour everything and leave the land
a waste. They were the harbingers, Joel said, of another
devastation, of another swarm of "locusts" with Jehovah at their head, punishing yet more terribly. Only a
day of national humiliation and prayer might prevent it.
They day was set. The prayers were offered. Jehovah
was persuaded, the people spared.

Immediately, Joel's prophetic stature shrinks. He
sees "Multitudes, multitudes [of the Gentile nations] in
the valley of decision . . ." with Jehovah judging, anni-
hilating them. Thankful that Jerusalem and Judah had
been spared, Joel was wild with rejoicing at the Gentiles' punishment. He bids the Jews beat their plowshares back into swords, their pruning-hooks into
spears, to fight again!

He moved in a little world, ruled by a little Jehovah.
He never sensed the universality of God's grace, never
rebuked sin with the greater prophets. One tiny ray of
light creeps from his prophecy; he hears Jehovah say, "I
will pour out my Spirit upon all flesh; and your sons and
daughters shall prophesy, your old men shall dream
dreams, your young men shall see visions."

Better visions, Joel, than yours?

*Joel 1:15 ff.; 2:15 ff.; 3:14 ff.; 2:28.*

# Jonah

HE LAY THREE DAYS AND NIGHTS IN THE BELLY OF A whale. No, of a "big fish." Jonah's fish is more bothersome than Daniel's lions, dwarfing again the man, confusing again the message. The fish is not the story; just part of the story's furniture.

He was the son of Amittai, born at Gath-hepher (an hour's walk from Nazareth), sent by God to preach in Nineveh. He rebelled. He ran . . . westward, away. He ran into a storm; the sailors threw him overboard; the great fish came. . . . Then Jonah went on to Nineveh, preached so convincingly that the whole city donned sackcloth and repented!

We argue like children over the dimensions of the stomach of the fish, or over who wrote Jonah's Book! Why? The teaching of Jonah is so painfully clear: No man can find a hideaway from conscience, nor from God. . . . No nation, knowing God, dare keep Him to themselves. . . . Nineveh must know God too . . . the heathen heart is as able to find, hold, God as is the orthodox.

God was rebuking not only the gracelessness of Jonah, but the exclusiveness and bigotry of the Jew. Those who know must preach . . . there is a teaching, evangelizing obligation. . . .

The *missionary obligation!*

*II Kings 14:25; Jonah 1:1 ff.; 3:1 ff.*

# *Malachi*

MALACHI IS THE LAST OF THE PROPHETS, THE LAST MAN of the Old Testament. He is the seal, the climax, the end of them. He stands in a darkening doorway, in the falling dusk of a night which is to be four centuries long. But yonder Malachi sees the dawn, in which walks the Son of Man.

He condemns the same sins and people as his predecessors. In two aspects he overreaches them. The worship of the heathen, if it be sincere, he says, is acceptable to the one great, universal God. And he detests haphazard marriage and divorce. Malachi is the champion of the home. There faith, he knows, begins, or there it early dies. He fights for wholesome, fireside love, for prayers at mothers' knees, for fidelity life-long. The fate of a nation, he realizes, depends on the fate of its homes. We should study Malachi; one in seven of our marriages ends in divorce court; the keeping of the home is one of our lost arts.

> "Sunset and evening star,
> And one clear call. . . ."

It was a plaintive note for the postlude of prophecy to end upon, a tremblingly beautiful note to hang in the long dark night.

*Malachi 1:11; 2:11 ff.; 3:16 ff.*

185

# Zacharias

OVER IN HEROD'S TEMPLE MOVED A PRIEST WELL stricken in years; Zacharias took his turn at altar duties, reading faithfully his Scriptures, firm in the old faith that some day the Deliverer would come.

Honor and glory gurst upon him in old age. Selected by lot one day to carry the fire from the outer altar of burnt-offering to the golden altar of incense in the inner Holy Place (once in a lifetime, that happened!), he heard an angel speak: ". . . thy wife Elizabeth shall bear thee a son, and thou shalt call his name John . . . and he shall . . . make ready for the Lord a people prepared for him. . . ."

Abraham had laughed at such a greeting. Zacharias did not laugh; he was bewildered. He and Elizabeth were so old. . . . How. . . . For only that Zacharias was struck speechless, dumb.

But speech, nay, song broke from his lips again the day he took the child to be circumcised. Understanding now, Zacharias sang the "Benedictus," that epic of sacred harmony which we sing across Christendom today.

What a gamut of emotions, of puzzlement, despair, and joy, for the last days of an old man!

*Luke 1:5 ff.; 67 ff.*

# *Elizabeth*

ELIZABETH, WIFE OF ZACHARIAS, WAS A MASTERPIECE of the handiwork of God. She was righteous. She was blameless. She was sad. All life long she had wanted a child. (What woman does not?) When the babe foretold by Gabriel moved at last in her womb, her spirit touched the pinnacles of heaven. It was true, then! This *was* to be John, the Preparer, a Nazirite like Samson, Samuel, filled with the Holy Spirit even from his mother's womb.

One day a cousin, Mary, came to visit her. Mary was young. She too had talked with Gabriel; she too would have a child. Then Elizabeth "lifted up her voice with a loud cry." The mother of the Lord had come to her own house! There they sat, youth and age, together . . . Mary, mother of Jesus, Elizabeth, mother of John . . . talking in whispers . . . smiling, weeping, brooding, anticipating . . . Mary . . . and Elizabeth.

All too soon their happiness took wings. They and their unborn babes were to suffer much. Elizabeth, likely, was dead before her John died in Herod's prison. But Mary was to climb Calvary with her Jesus and the thieves.

*Luke 1:6 ff., 15, 42 ff.*

# John the Baptist

HE WAS THE FIRST CHRISTIAN, THE MORNING STAR OF the Kingdom of God. Like Elijah, like Amos, he was Tekoa-bred; he came out of the desert wilder than Ishmael, preaching wildly, enveloped in blue fire. "Prepare ye ... repent ye ... The Kingdom of God is at hand ..." A voice crying in the wilderness, clearing the way for the Conqueror.

John baptized (hence, "The Baptist") in the Jordan, using water to wash away sin. One would soon come to baptize them with the Holy Ghost instead of water. The One came ... came to John the Baptist to be baptized: "Behold," cries John, "the Lamb of God, which taketh away the sin of the world." The child of Mary, the child of Elizabeth ... knee-deep in Jordan ... together. Then John vanishes.

Years later, fast in Herod's dungeon, doubt slipped a fetter on his soul. He asks of Jesus, "Art thou He that should come, or ..." But when he hears of the work of Jesus, he is the militant Baptist again. He is glad to die. ... Salome sends a charger ... the executioner comes through the dungeon door ... the morning star fades brilliantly into the sunrise.

*Matthew 3:1 ff.; 13 ff.; 11:2 ff.; Mark 6:14 ff;*
*John 1:29.*

# *Joseph of Nazareth*

WHY ARE THE RECORDS SO MEAGER? WHY DO THEY NOT tell more? Why must the father of Jesus be concealed by unjust silence? Or would he, great heart that he was, want it that way?

Joseph was industrious. Humble laborer, descendant of King David, he spent his long days happily in his Nazareth shop, planing cedars from Lebanon, sawing hard woods from the hills. He passed the habit of stern labor to the Son apprenticed at his side.

He was kindly. Betrothed to Mary and discovering her condition, he planned first quietly to disown her, but found that he could not. He took her down to Bethlehem to keep her away from the gossip of the town. He marveled with her at this Son, poured his life, his hope, his kindliness into the little breast of the Prince of Kindliness.

He was pious. He took Mary and the Babe regularly, each year, to the Temple feasts. Once, when they lost him in the Passover crowd, Joseph was frantic.

This is the last we hear of Joseph. He may have died when Jesus was eighteen. Jesus never talked of him. But Jesus was industrious, kindly, and pious. Did father Joseph give him these?

*Matt. 1:18 f.; 13:55; Luke 2:4, 41 ff.*

# Mary of Nazareth

SHE KNEW THE FARTHEST HEIGHTS OF JOY, THE DEEP-est vale of tears. Mary, the mother of Jesus, was Mary, mother of joy, when she learned He was to come. She sang then the "Magnificat"—"My soul doth magnify the Lord. . . ." Clutching him in the Bethlehem straw, she listened with closed eyes to the angel's song, turned his wee face to see the star. When she lost him that day in Jerusalem, she was afraid, lest he be gone forever.

As he grew she believed in him; at the wedding in Cana she bade the servants, "Whatsoever he saith unto you, do it." But afterward, on the edge of a surly crowd, she feared for him, begged him to leave his preaching and come home to her before they killed him. He could not come. It was the parting of the ways.

Still she followed, from afar, anguished, praying, hoping, but never again interfering. At last she saw his arms stretched wide, a brutal Roman soldier driving nails. . . . Out of the night she heard him say to John, "Behold thy mother."

Some worship her, and some adore. All the world stands mute before her peaceful, patient face. Mary, mother of Jesus. Mary, mother of love.

*Mark 3:21, 32; Luke 1:46 ff.; 2:19, 48;*
*John 2:5; 19:27.*

# *Jesus*

JESUS, SON OF MARY, WAS OF HER BUT NOT HERS. HE was God's, wholly. He is the greatest soul of time, arrived in time's fulness to breathe into the corpse of a dead humanity a resurrecting, life-restoring Spirit, giving it direction and abundance, to realize its heavenly origin and divine destination. In his person humanity swept up to a new high-water mark.

He was Teacher, putting to blush Plato and Socrates, for in him was all the prophets' teaching, all the truth of all religions, and more. He added a rare finale to teaching: he lived it. He practiced the Sermon on the Mount before He preached it.

He was Physician, causing the lame to walk in a new strength, the strength of God; he gave mankind new ears, tuned to hear the whispering voice of a new God; he struck the scales from men's blind eyes, brought God walking to them in their darkness, across the sweet wide meadows of hope.

He was Master of Life, glorifying its commonplace, setting every common bush along the wayside afire with God. Master of Death, he snapped the terror of death and made it victory, that we might never fear to die.

Men misunderstood him and crucified him. Our world would do the same if He came back.

*Mark 1:22; Matt. 11:4 f.; Luke 19:10;*
*John 11:25; I Cor. 2:8; Galatians 4:4.*

# Simeon

MARY AND JOSEPH, JUST AND DEVOUT, TOOK THEIR BABE
soon to Jerusalem to present him to God. At the Temple door they met a man more just and devout than
they. Proudly Mary gave her baby into the arms of aged
Simeon, and Simeon, with glistening eye and heart
aburst, turned to the altar to give him to God.

All his life the old man had waited for this hour.
Promised a glimpse of the coming Messiah before he
died, he had held the hope while others let it go. It was
a long, lonely vigil, and at times it seemed that it must
fail. Then . . . Mary came. Song undying broke from
Simeon's lips; he sang the "Nunc Dimittis"—"Lord, now
lettest thou thy servant depart in peace." He could die
now. In his own arms he had held Christ, the Lord.

Since the fourth century, the "Nunc Dimittis" has
been the evensong of the church. Since then, too, the
ministers of Christ have offered babyhood to God at
their altars, with the ebullient joy of Simeon blowing
tempests in their souls.

*Luke 2:22 ff.*

# *Anna*

AGED PROPHETESS ANNA STOOD AT THE SIDE OF AGED prophet Simeon as he sang. She had been seven years a wife, eighty-four a widow, a hundred years a dreamer of that godly remnant which constantly searched the skies through the intertestamental night for the rising of the Messiah's star. It was her hour as well as Simeon's. She knew, too, that this was He who should come.

Her presence that day proved that prophecy had spanned the gap between Malachi and the Baptist, that the prophetess blood of Miriam and Deborah had not perished from the earth.

She grew old gracefully. The slow passing of the years could not snap in her the silver cord of hope nor shatter the golden bowl of faith. She is one of Timothy's "widows, indeed," who, denied the triumphs of mother-hood, gave herself to the good works of pity and piety. You may meet her on the street, some day, in the hood of a Sister of Charity or in the black cap of a Deaconess.

*Luke 2:36 ff.*

# Andrew

"AND HE APPOINTED TWELVE . . ." THE GLORIOUS COMpany of the Apostles. *The* Twelve, whose lives are deathless!

The first appointed was Andrew, who had heard the Baptist preach. He was the first missionary of the Kingdom of Heaven, the first "personal worker" in Christ's Church.

Andrew was forever bringing some one. He brought, first, his own brother. Bravo, Andrew! It is easier to preach to the heathen than to one's own kin. Andrew brought Peter to Jesus, and stepped humbly aside as Peter rose to second-in-command.

He brought a little lad to Jesus, a lad with two fishes and five loaves, a lad with resources. "There is a lad here . . ." he said to Christ. (Moody was discovered in a shoe-shop, Billy Sunday on a baseball diamond, Livingstone at a spinning-jenny. Lads with resources, they were! Some one found them there, some Andrew said, "There is a lad here . . .")

Certain Greeks came, perplexed, investigating, asking, "Sir, we would see Jesus." Andrew led them in. The first Apostle to the Gentiles!

No miracles. No great resounding sermons. But would God he were here today! A sick humanity is crying, "Sir, we would see Jesus." And a perplexed, resourceful, investigating youth awaits an inspired introducer, saying, "There is a lad here . . ."

*Mark 3:14; John 1:40 ff.; 6:8; 12:20 ff.*

# *Peter*

PETER'S SOUL WAS A SURGING TIDE; NOW HIGH, TEM-
pestuous, crashing like the waves on Galilee; now low,
receding, caught in the backwash of doubt, spent on the
shores of fear. He rocked like a skyscraper in a gale;
skyscraper-like, too, he pointed ever heavenward, came
back ever to dead center when the gale had passed. He
was rooted deep in the bedrock of the Spirit; nay, his
spirit *was* the Rock on which Christ built his Church.

He forsook all to follow Christ; he leaped into the
sea, tried walking on deep waters in a tempest at
Christ's call; the day after Calvary he returned to his
nets. He wanted to die for Christ; a servant-girl laughed
and he changed his mind. In the fell clutch of circum-
stance he was weak; in the grip of the Great Conviction
he cried, "Thou art the Christ!"

The Spirit won him at last. The salty, fighting hands
of the cursing fisherman became the healing hands of
the saint; even nailed to a cross, they signal to the after-
ages his Apostolic Benediction.

Peter was the most human of the Twelve and the
most valuable to Christ; a diamond in the rough, with
great polishing possibilities. He was transfigured and
transformed. He developed.

*Matt. 14:28 ff.; 16:16 ff.; Mark 14:66 ff.; Luke*
*5:11; John 13:37, 21:3.*

# Philip

HE WAS PHILIP THE PLODDER, A SLOW, PROSAIC, DIFFI-dent, matter-of-fact machine. To know him is to know how patient Jesus was.

He never fully knew his Lord; in the midst of that breathless sermon in the 14th of John he blurted out: "Lord, *show* us the Father!" He never fully felt the thrust of Jesus' power. When the five thousand waited to be fed, he thought not of Christ's potency, but of absent caterers: "Two hundred pennyworth of bread is not sufficient. . . ." When the Greeks came seeking Jesus, Philip could not think what to do. Should *foreigners* be led to Jesus Christ? He turned them over to Andrew!

His fellows walked in close camaraderie with Christ; Philip never quite caught step. He never would testify in prayer-meeting, were he here now, nor lead a great revival. But he would be one of those gallant plodders (may their tribe increase!) who are always on hand to set up tables for a church supper, or teach as substitute teacher in the Sunday school, or bring another Nathanael in. He plodded on faithfully, teaching, preaching, to a martyr's grave in Hierapolis, seeing darkly, through a glass, to the end. Perhaps, for that very reason, he was a greater martyr than those who saw clearly.

*John 1:44 ff.; 6:7; 12:21 ff.; 14:8.*

# *Nathanael*

JESUS PAID HIM A HIGH COMPLIMENT: "BEHOLD AN
Israelite indeed, in whom is no guile." That was a shock
to Nathanael, for he had just been laughing at Jesus.
Told by Philip that the Nazarene was the expected Messiah, he sneered: "Can there any good thing come out
of Nazareth?" And Philip, ready for once, flashed back,
"Come and see." He came. He saw. He was conquered.
One look at that wondrous countenance, and his sneer
was gone: "Thou *art* the Son of God."

Aye, Philip, good *does* come from lowly Nazareths.
Presidents have come out of log cabins; artists and
poets are born in Mott Street and Mulberry Bend;
saints move up from Shantytown to sit with God.
Towns mean nothing; birthplaces make poor identifica-
tion tags. Left to himself and his environment, man is
worth little or nothing. But let the love of God reach for
a man and find him, in Nazareth or Pittsburgh or Bom-
bay, and that man is beatified.

Nathanael the Convinced! He spent the rest of his
life touching men with the love of God in a thousand little towns we never heard of and never shall.

*John 1:45 ff.*

# Nicodemus

HE MOVED AT NIGHT, LIKE A FRIGHTENED BIRD. TOO brave for cowardice and too hesitant for heroism, he sought the cover of doubt's darkness whenever God's light threatened him. Nicodemus was the Night Disciple, the apostle of honest questioning and stalemated intellect.

He sat once with Jesus at midnight, on a Jerusalem housetop, talking of miracles, of being born again. Jesus almost won him there; Nicodemus stood within an inch of the Kingdom. Then he backed off into darkness again. So near and yet so far!

When his Sanhedrin clamored for Jesus' arrest and execution, Nicodemus, unstrung, tried feebly to stop it: "Doth our law judge any man before it hear him? . . ."

Only after the Crucifixion did he throw his cloak of fear into the arms of night and step boldly forth to meet the light. He came with Arimathean Joseph to take Christ's body down and give it kingly burial. Too late, Nicodemus! Like roses at a funeral, that gesture was an apology for neglected friendship.

Night still holds him in her sullen shroud. Is he uncomfortable there? Does he rebuke his soul with the words once addressed by a pupil to the memory of Matthew Arnold, "The mark of that man is on me yet"?

*John 3:1 ff.; 7:51; 19:38 ff.*

# James, Son of Zebedee

STILL WATERS RUN DEEP. EDISON AND BONAPARTE talked little, yet the Little Corporal shook the earth and the Wizard lighted it. James, son of Zebedee, was a quietist. While Peter and Thomas boasted, James was exasperatingly silent. He never bragged, nor did he ever deny.

When he did speak, he invariably said the wrong thing. Once he suggested setting fire to an inhospitable village; once he asked for a prominent seat in Christ's kingdom. He was young, interested, in a hurry. Jesus smilingly dubbed him one of "the sons of thunder."

He was as silent as Gibraltar, and as strong. When the testing-hour came, James was the first to drink (how happily he drank!) of the bitter cup of death. Herod killed him. Herod hated him. He was too quiet.

Did James and Jesus walk for hours in Galilee and never speak a single word? Why not? Cousins in the flesh, closer than brothers in the spirit, between them was that rare flash of understanding which only two kindred souls can know.

Whenever Jesus needed the support of an understanding heart (in Jairus' house, on Transfiguration's Mount, in moonlit Gethsemane) he took with him James the Silent, the mute, sustaining Coöperator.

*Matt. 17:1; Acts 12:2; Mark 3:17; 10:35 ff.;*
*14:33; Luke 8:51; 9:54 ff.*

# John

HE MOVED ABOUT IN A CHARMED CIRCLE OF LOVE. Pious parents named him John ("one whom Jehovah loves") and the Fourth Gospel calls him "that Disciple whom Jesus loved." He justified the faith of both Christ and Zebedee.

In love he left his nets floating on Galilee to fish with Christ for men; in love he helped arrange the perilous Last Supper; in love he stood at the Cross (the only disciple there!) and heard Jesus commend Mother Mary to his care; in love he ran to the empty tomb in the first whispers of Easter's holy dawn; in love he was the first to recognize the risen Master walking on old Tiberias' shore. In love he built the first church at Jerusalem, and churches in Ephesus and Asia Minor. He wrote a best-seller: the loveliest and most popular Life of Jesus Christ.

If you would know the nature of God, know Jesus Christ: He is a Christlike God. And would you know what Christ was like? Then study John, the most Christlike Apostle, the Galahad of the Round Table of the Twelve.

*Luke 5:11; John 19:26 f.; 20:2; 21:7;*
*Acts 4:13 ff.*

# Matthew

HE SOLD HIMSELF TWICE, ONCE TO MAMMON AND ONCE to God. He began as a publican, a despised tax-collector for the Romans, bleeding his people white to satisfy the insatiable thirst of Rome for gold, whiter yet to build, by way of honest graft, a fortune for himself. Rome despised him; Jewry hated him. Matthew was rich and wretched.

Then the Master spoke, saying, simply. "Follow me." Instantly he left his thieving, exchanged his publican wretchedness for apostolic dignity, deserted wealth and mammon for Christ and honesty. He even arranged a banquet of his old publican cronies, at which Jesus was chief speaker. Society talked and prejudice flared, but Jesus did it just the same. He was not come to save the righteous, but sinners to repentance.

"Ye *cannot* serve God and mammon," says Matthew. How he knew whereof he spoke! "It is easier for a camel to go through the eye of a needle than . . ." Now you know how hard was the coming of Matthew, how rich his reward at the end.

"Once a thief, always a thief." Who started that? Here is a thief become minister, a pygmy character become Colossus of the Saints.

*Matt. 6:24; 9:9 ff.; 19:24.*

# *Thomas*

JESUS WAS FAIR WITH THOMAS; MOST OF US ARE CRUEL. Jesus saw his strength; we see his weaknesses. To us he is Thomas the Doubter, always whining, "Lord, we know not . . . ," believing only when he could touch his finger to the nailprints, lay his hand in the spear-wound in the side. Jesus saw in Thomas not only a man slow to believe, moody, gloomy, seeing too much the difficulties of faith, but an honest mind and heroic heart as well. "Let us also go, that we may die with him," bade Thomas when danger threatened Christ. Jesus liked that, rewarded it: "Reach hither thy finger. . . ." Jesus never dodged a doubter nor condemned a critic, anywhere. Why should we?

Thomas only wanted to *know* that he knew. Is that sin? If it is, it is usable sin. Didymus was an asset to the band, a check rein of reason on the capricious emotions of Peter and Zelotes. He is highly usable to us. Many a preacher would be a better preacher were there a liberal sprinkling of doubting Thomases in his pews; many a self-conscious saint would be a better saint were he to understand that frank questioning is far better than untried, dogmatic faith, that it is but part of man's

". . . keen, enormous, haunting, never-sated thirst for God."

*John 11:16; 14:5; 20:24 ff.*

# James, Son of Alpheus

THEY CALLED HIM "JAMES THE LITTLE" TO DISTINGUISH
him from Zebedee's James, who was taller. Like all
nicknames, it was criminally unfair. Steinmetz was short
of stature. So were Napoleon, and Julius Caesar, and
Charles Lamb.

His mother was one of the three Marys who came to
Calvary. He had a brother Joses, a believer. Alpheus,
his father, may also have been Alpheus, father of
Matthew. If that be true, it was a royal family; it gave to
the Kingdom a father, a mother, and three sons.

James the Little was their scion, spiritually. Jesus had
no contempt for littleness; he depended on it. He talked
of little mustard seeds and little lost coins; he built his
hope on the faith of little men. He had among his Apostles not one single famous name, not one millionaire, or
ruler, or college president. His Church has been main-
tained, for nineteen hundred years, on widows' mites
and orphans' farthings, a penny here, a penny there; on
the labors of little cobblers like Carey, little cripples like
Fanny Crosby. "Little" men are the kingdom's corner-
stones; take them out and the whole thing would collapse.

James the Little, indeed!

*Matt. 10:3; 27:56; Mark 2:14.*

# *Simon Zelotes*

STUDY HIS FACE IN DA VINCI'S "LAST SUPPER"; HERE IS a jaw set hard, eyes of blue steel, nervous hands ready to fly into fists; Simon, the Zealot, the "flaming one." But yesterday he preached revolt, talked crazily of going to war with Rome! Let the Herodians connive, and the Pharisees submit. For himself and his Zealots the sword! Peaceful resolution! Too slow. Death to them. He might be killed in the attempt, but what of that? He'd die regretting that he had but one life to give.

Jesus took him—*him*—into the Band. Odd? No! Any crusade needs "flaming ones" who never count the cost. James the Silent and John the Beloved, mystics, lovers, needed a flame, for balance's sake. . . .

But Simon the Apostle was far different from Simon the (political) Zealot. The advocate of armed revolt became the Apostle of God's love; Jesus had put the flame in harness. The fitful, spontaneous blaze settled down into the steady, mature heat of a bed of glowing coals.

Why must we argue stupidly about Christ's miracles? Long centuries gone from us, he still changes characters, rebuilds lives; even yet he harnesses erratic, flaming spirits to do God's will.

*Luke 6:15.*

# Thaddeus

HE HAD THREE NAMES. THE FIRST WAS A HANDICAP; IT was Judas. Whenever the Gospel writers mention it, they are quick to assure us that this was "*not* Iscariot." The second was Lebbeus; that was given to him as a baby, when he could neither approve nor reject. The third was Thaddeus; his companions called him that; it means "great-heart." He earned it.

With Thomas and Philip, he gained fame as a sermon heckler in John 14—"Lord, how is it that thou wilt manifest thyself unto us, and not unto the world?" Why are so few to gain the inner courts of God? Was this Kingdom to be exclusive or inclusive, democratic or aristocratic? "If a man love me . . . ," answered Jesus, ". . . my Father will love him, and we will come unto him."

Great-heart is right! That brave question cleared the road to heaven for many of us. It makes us see that those who dwell with God are no exclusive sect or set, that *any* man, if he obey love's discipline, may enter in. Any man! Any Englishman, Frenchman, Chinese:

Great-heart! A heart big enough to want to embrace all humanity.

*Matt. 10:3; John 14:22 f.*

# Judas Iscariot

ISCARIOT! THE HISS OF A SNAKE IS HIDDEN IN THE NAME. He is the only one of the Twelve *not* a Galilean; the only one appointed to office (and disgracing it); the only one to obey his baser impulses and die outlawed from God.

His whole discipleship was one grand accumulation of disillusionment and mistake. Looking ahead to promotion when Christ established his Kingdom, his resentment smoldered and grew as the setting-up was continuously postponed. Perhaps he only wanted to force the issue by placing Christ in crisis; perhaps he only wanted Christ himself to prove that he was the Messiah and not a charlatan; perhaps he knew that Christ risen would overcome the world. Perhaps . . . but why perhaps? There are a thousand perhaps, a million excuses yet unoffered for Judas. The fact remains that while miracles of character-transformation were worked in eleven disciples, this twelfth, this man of Kerioth, remained unchanged. Judas was The-Man-Who-Might-Have-Been.

He thought to sell his Lord, but succeeded only in selling himself. He thought to find forgetfulness in suicide; he should have sought mercy at the Cross. It was there, waiting. But . . . no . . . he was just The-Man-Who-Might-Have-Been.

*Matt. 10:4; 26:14 ff.; 27:3 ff.; John 12:6; 13:29.*

# Mary Magdalene

WE HAVE HAD HER IN THE PILLORY FOR NINETEEN hundred years, flinging mud; *we* should have been pilloried. This Mary was never a harlot; there is no evidence, anywhere, for that. At most she was a neurotic, obsessed by intense depression or morbid melancholy. At best she was a loving follower of the Band, ministering, with Joanna and Susanna, to the needs of him who had not where to lay his head.

Yes, Jesus "cast seven devils" from her; he gave her happiness and content, joy and a task to dispel her introspection and depression, the certainty of love to outwit melancholy.

She followed him adown the Galilean road, thrilling at his words and works, trembling at the growing hostility of the crowd. She followed him up Calvary, saw nails bite into the hands which once had lifted her, a spear thrust for the heart that beat with hers. She supported stricken Mother Mary, led her away when it was done, and returned with spices for the burial.

Though the tomb door was sealed, she never believed that he could go. In the garden, at dawn, she sat among the lilies, weeping, waiting. Behind her a voice, low, sweet: "Mary!"

She had never doubted it. Had he not come when *she* was dead, and made her life as bright again as the singing of a lark?

*Matt. 27:55 f.; Mark 15:47; 16 f.; Luke 8:2 f.;*
*John 19:25; 20:1 ff.*

# *Joanna*

SHE MUST HAVE BEEN A FRIEND OF MARY MAGDA-
lene's. They did things together. They had both been
healed of "evil spirits and infirmities"; both ministered
to him while he lived, both helped anoint his body when
he died, both ran to tell the good news of his resurrection. A strange friendship. Like the friendship of the
prince and the pauper in Mark Twain. The Magdalene
was a commoner, while Joanna was wife of Chuza, a
steward in the house of Herod Antipas, a "saint in Caesar's household" where sainthood was hard.

She "ministered unto him of her substance." What
might that mean? Food? Shelter? Pieces of silver, gold?
Why may it not also mean that Joanna gave him of her
spiritual substance, that she preached Christ in the
kitchens of Antipas, stood for him in the courtyard or
the harem while Chuza, half-heartedly sympathetic,
gave his attention to other things—to being a good
steward to Herod? Joanna was God's steward.

Some day, some church with courage will put up a
bronze plaque, reading, "This church erected and main-
tained by its men (devotion, 50%) and by its Ladies'
Aid Society (devotion, 100%)."

*Luke 8:3; 24:10.*

208

# *Joses*

JESUS HAD FOUR BROTHERS. TWO OF THEM DID YEOMAN
service in His Church; the other two did nothing. Joses
and Simon were just brothers. They never did a thing,
nor said a thing, worth recording. They just stayed
home, haunting their father's footsteps in the old carpenter shop. They were too busy making ox-yokes and
well-buckets for the farmers to pay much attention to
their dreamy-eyed brother. There was money in ox-
yokes. And who wanted to be a wandering mendicant,
anyway?

Poet Harry Kemp puts it this way:

"Of all the mistakes of the ages, the saddest, methinks,
    was this,
  To have such a brother as Jesus, to speak with him,
    day by day,
  But never to catch the vision which glorified his clay."

We dare not judge Joses, lest we be judged. We have
had this Elder Brother with us now for many a century,
but not one in a thousand has ever really known him,
ever really caught . . .

*Mark 6:3.*

# James, Brother of Jesus

HE GREW UP IN THE SAME HOUSE WITH JESUS CHRIST, but they were miles apart. Not until after Easter Day did James completely understand; then he gave himself, mind, body, heart, and soul to the Cause. He became Bishop of Jerusalem, a power—the power—in the first church. Three times Paul came to him for advice.

His knees, men said, were calloused as a camel's from long praying. The Scribes and Pharisees were afraid of a man like that; they threw him from a Temple pinnacle to death. Thus, by works and faith, the brother doubter became a saint in his own right.

He wrote a great Epistle. It reads like his Brother's Sermon on the Mount. Handle it carefully. It's explosive. It is a gospel of good works, saying nothing of doctrine, much about character. It is beclouded by no dull theology; it is simple, straightforward street-corner Christianity. If we had more of it, we'd have a better world.

Brother James was humble. He never signed himself "James, brother of Jesus," but always, "James, the servant of the Lord Jesus Christ!"

*Mark 6:3; Acts 12:17; 15:4; 21:18; Gal. 1:19; 2:9; James 1:1.*

# Jude

JUDE, AS A BROTHER, STOOD HALFWAY BETWEEN JOSES and James. Like Joses, it was hard for him to get what Jesus was driving at; like James, he got it only after Jesus died. He was proud of his brother James: he copied him in signing himself, "Jude, the servant of Jesus Christ, and brother of James"!

He never attained the high position of his brother in the church. Perhaps he never wanted it. "Bishop" is a pretty title, but a most unpleasant, unattractive job. But when he preached or wrote, he was like the prophets of old. His words drip vitriol. His little Book, slipped in at the Bible's end, is a masterpiece. He wrote it in contention for "the faith once delivered to the saints." Heresies had risen, false teachers were abroad, using false faith as a cloak for vice. Jude tore that cloak to pieces. Between his lines we may find a familiar figure, if we search—a Man with a whip of cords cleansing the Temple. . . .

Jesus, James, and Jude! A trinity of courage, simplicity, and truth. Did ever any other mother have three such sons before? Or since?

*Mark 6:3; John 2:13 ff.; Jude 1, 3.*

# *Martha*

TWO SISTERS LIVED AT BETHANY, IN A FRIENDLY HOUSE at the side of the road which the Son of Man knew well. Their latch-string was always out, their table always set for passers-by. Martha saw to that.

She had a careful mind and a troubled heart. Things, like latch-strings and tables, worried her. She had a temper; she lost it that day when Jesus came to supper at her house and Mary sat at his feet, doing nothing, while *she* prepared the meal. "Lord . . . bid her . . . that she help me."

Housewives love her for that, "practical" folks bless her. It's all right to dream, to preach, to meditate, they say, but some one must set the table, some one must do the work! They forget that there are different kinds of food—and work.

Too, they miss that other Martha, the rejuvenated Martha who accepted Jesus' rebuke that day, and ceased forever to be overanxious over things. When Lazarus died and Jesus returned to Bethany, Martha ran down the road to meet him, to confess her love and faith, while Mary "sat still in the house," crushed. And when Mary anointed his feet, at another banquet, Martha did *not* complain. By this time she herself had chosen the better part, which would not be taken from her.

*Luke 10:38 ff.; John 11:20; 12:2 ff.*

# Mary of Bethany

FEAST UPON HER IN YOUR HEARTS, ALL YE WHO LOVE the Lord. This is the Mary of the Feasts. At Martha's feast she sat at Jesus' feet as his disciple, reading his thoughts, his innermost desire, giving him the joy of human fellowship. At the feast before the Passion, she knelt at his feet in tearful gratitude. She spilled more than perfume over his feet that day. She poured out all the love of a broken, loving heart.

She knew what Martha did not know, that it is easier to provide food for a feast than ease and companionship for a guest. She wanted, as much as her sister, to minister to the Guest. She knew how weary he was, and she gave him rest; she knew his soul's hunger, and she fed it. She knew him better than Martha, and so she served him best.

She knew him better! Better than even his own disciples knew him, than his own mother, brothers, sisters, knew him. His own rejected him, but Mary welcomed him.

Is there a man among us who thinks that he can serve the Lord until he knows him? Until he has sat, or knelt, or fallen, with Mary, at his feet?

*Luke 10:39; John 12:3.*

# *Lazarus the Beggar*

THE BEGGAR LAZARUS SAT AT DIVES' GATE, IN RAGS AND full of sores, fighting dogs for crumbs from the rich man's board. Then the both of them died. Lazarus rested in Abraham's bosom. Dives languished in Hades, below, begging a cool drop of water on his tongue. Abraham was merciless; there was no drop of water now for one who had begrudged a few crumbs.

Millions drowning in poverty have grasped at this story as sinking men grasp at straws. They should not. Jesus is not teaching here that the poor are saved because they are poor, nor the rich doomed because they are rich; this is no superficial attempt to "make things even in the next world." Lazarus was rewarded because he had found his help and sustenance in God. Dives' suffering was the result of his selfishness; he had used his wealth unwisely, had *not* made to himself friends of the mammon of unrighteousness.

Dives reformed in Hades. Too late, yes, but better late than never. He begged that word be sent to his five living brothers, that they might be warned of his plight and mend their ways.

So hell, as well as heaven, hath her miracles!

*Luke 16:19 ff.*

# *Lazarus of Bethany*

JESUS AND LAZARUS WERE CLOSE FRIENDS; JESUS LET Lazarus die when he might have saved him. It was done purposely, to demonstrate Christ's power over death.

Jerusalem, impenitent and scornful, needed a lesson; disciples in embryo were dubious; enemies were watching their chance. An indisputable manifestation was imperative. Jesus waited until Lazarus was actually dead. Then he raised him.

The effects of the miracle were immediate catastrophe and ultimate triumph. The rulers, frantic in defeat, convened the Sanhedrin and resolved to kill him. But a multitude, inspired, cheered and sang at the Triumphal Entry. A divine time-defying optimism had captured men: death had been robbed of its sting, the grave of its victory.

Lazarus disappears soon after the miracle. No, he keeps coming back. He has reappeared at the bier of every Christian gone in death, to dry tears and heal the broken-hearted with the words addressed by Christ to Martha: "Thy brother shall rise again!" Thy brother . . . mother . . . father . . . child shall rise again.

It was a friendship born in heaven, meant for earth. Jesus and Lazarus, divine conspirators, friends of men, have made us friends with death.

*John 11:1 ff.; 12:9 ff.*

# *Bartimæus*

"ALMS, ALMS! FOR THE LOVE OF ALLAH, ALMS!" CRY
the beggars of Araby. "Alms, alms," cried blind beggar
Bartimæus, crouching by the highway down which
came the pilgrims to Passover, among them Jesus
Christ. The crowd pushed close to look upon the
wonder-working Nazarene, and Bartimæus, hearing
with sharpened ears what he could not see with dead-
ened eyes, fought his way through the press. Jesus of
Nazareth was passing by! He might never pass this way
again. Dropping his cloak (the one thing he owned)
Bartimæus clawed or crawled to the feet of the Master.
"Jesus . . . have mercy on me!" Not a common tramp
seeking coins, but a sufferer seeking sight. His persisten-
cy proved his faith. Jesus healed him with a word.

Bartimæus never went back to reclaim his beggar's
rags; he never squatted in the dust again; he followed
Christ. His world was brilliant now; he saw things he
had been blind to all his life.

Did your eyes burn, Bartimæus, when you saw
Christ on the Cross? Were they opened that you might
see *that?*

*Mark 10:46 ff.; Luke 18:35-43.*

# Zacchaeus

JERICHO WAS THE FRUITFUL PANTRY OF JUDEA, A CITY
of tax-gatherers and priests. The priests hated Jesus and
the populace hated the publicans. Jesus defied them
both by supping at the house of Zacchæus, the most despised publican in town.

Now Zacchæus was another "little" man; he could
never see anything in a crowd. So he ran ahead of the
crowd, when Jesus came to Jericho, and shinned up a
sycamore tree. He *would* do that; Zacchæus had always
wanted to climb; he had a sick conscience and an unsat-
isfied soul and a heart that reached for better things.
Jesus saw him in the tree. "Zacchæus . . . come down;
for today I must abide at thy house." The little fellow
clambered down and they walked on together, Saviour
and profiteer! And behind the closed doors of his own
house Jesus introduced the publican to penitence, salvation, and peace.

Come down, Zacchæus! Come down out of it, man,
down out of your screening leaves of hesitancy, and
walk with Jesus Christ. Climb down and give your
climbing soul a chance.

*Luke 19:1 ff.*

# Malchus

LANTERNS FLASHED IN GETHSEMANE. SOLDIERS STUM-
bled and cursed in the darkness; Jesus stood waiting, his
white robe glimmering beneath the olive trees. Just as
they saw him and rushed for him, Peter, roused from
deep sleep, leaped to his feet with a sword in his hand.
They had laid their uncouth hands upon the Christ!
Half asleep and swinging wildly, he struck the right ear
from the head of Malchus, high priest's servant and
idler, come to see the man-hunt and shout at the arrest.

Jesus, says Luke (physician!) healed the severed ear.
What did you think then, Malchus? You came to see
them strike him down; he turned to stop your pain.
What did you think when you saw him writhe on
Calvary?

"Put up thy sword . . . ," he commanded Peter.
Swords, even in defense, have no place in the Kingdom.
Put up thy sword, Christian, thy bayonet, machine-gun,
poison gas, or cease your idle cant of peace and brotherhood.

His ministry ended there, in Gethsemane, as he wanted it to end, in an act of compassion to an enemy and in
a word of rebuke for a great disciple, in one last, mighty
testimony of the power of love to conquer the sword.

*Luke 22:50 f.; John 18:1 ff.*

# *John Mark*

DOWN THROUGH THE SLEEPING CITY MARCHED THE
rabble-parade, with Jesus bound in their midst. Win-
dows flew open and faces peered out; a door flew open
and a young man stepped out, wrapped only in a bed-
sheet. The soldiers chased him; he ran, losing his sheet
in his flight. The crowd guffawed and moved on, leaving
young John Mark shivering in his hiding-place.

Later he appeared with Barnabas and Paul on their
first missionary journey, as their attendant or tour-man-
ager. Contention arose, and Mark deserted them. Paul
never forgot it; he refused to take Mark along on the
second tour. Spartan Paul tolerated no faint-hearted-
ness. Later Mark made good; then Paul loved him.

Early churchmen called him "Mark, the Stump-
fingered"; legends say his thumbs were slashed off by a
Roman sword that night he lost his sheet. True or no,
there was nothing stump-fingered about Mark when he
came to write his Gospel. His is the oldest, most vivid
and authentic Life of Christ. Matthew, Luke and John
copied from him liberally.

And remember this when you read it: Mark was interpreter, secretary, to Peter. He wrote down Peter's
reminiscences, being "careful not to leave out or falsify
anything."

A lukewarm missonary, but a remarkable historian.

*Mark 14:51 f.; Acts 12:25; 15:36 ff.;*
*II Timothy 4:11.*

# *Annas*

THEY "LED HIM AWAY TO ANNAS FIRST." TO OLD Annas, high priest emeritus now, retired from active service, but still directing things through his son-in-law, Caiaphas; to old Annas, who sat at the trials of Peter and John, whose five sons were also high priests, whose son, Annas, sentenced to death James, the Lord's brother.

Routed out of bed, he hurried down to question the Prisoner. There, with a mob outside and a ring of Roman steel around him, Jesus faced his real enemy at last. Annas *vs.* Chirst. Sadducee *vs.* Carpenter. Constituted authority *vs.* The World Made Flesh. Annas licked his thin lips and began.

He asked Jesus who his disciples were. His answer was a look of pitying scorn. Well, then, what doctrine was he teaching? "Ask them which heard me," challenged Jesus. A soldier slapped him for that, and Annas, the veteran cross-examiner, gave it up and bundled Jesus off to Caiaphas. He'd go back to bed now. Too old, anyway, for all this. Let Caiaphas handle it. Caiaphas was younger. Annas was tired. And beaten.

Did you sleep, old Annas?

*John 18:13 ff.; Acts 4:5 ff.; 12:1 ff.*

# Caiaphas

AT DAWN ON FRIDAY JESUS FACED THE SANHEDRIN. There was something owlish, wolfish, about them as they sat there, stroking their beards, eyes glinting like sparks in the new light, like the eyes of a wolf-pack closing in on its kill. In their center sat Caiaphas, a perpetual sneer astride his lips, Sadducee insolence in the pupils of his eyes; his long, thin, impatient fingers seemed already reaching across his table for the throat of the Nazarene. If any one man can be called the assassin of Jesus, that man is Caiaphas.

When he learned of the raising of Lazarus, he had started his pack in full howl. He resolved then to put Jesus out of the way, resolved it fitting that "one man should die for the people." Relentlessly he stalked his prey until this Friday's dawn. Then he finished it. He lied. He cheated. He swore false witnesses. He thrust aside shamelessly all rules of law, all forms of legal procedure. He talked slowly, soothingly; he raged, and tore his priestly robe to rags. He acted Hamlet, Lear, Macbeth, Othello, posed as devil's buffoon and shocked defender of God's truth. Jesus looked him in the eyes and said . . . nothing.

Caiaphas would have crucified his own mother, were she bothersome.

*Matt. 26:57 ff.; John 11:47 ff.*

# Pilate

HE HAD A GREAT RECORD AS CIVIL OFFICER: HE ALIEN-
ated everybody, did everything backwards. He marched
Roman troops through Jerusalem, bearing aloft their
idolatrous images; the Jews threatened to kill him. He
set up in Herod's palace tablets dedicated to emperor-
worship; Tiberius intervened to save his life. He dipped
his hands in the Temple treasury to build an aqueduct;
a bloody riot broke out. He staged a massacre of Gali-
leans, another of Samaritans. Then Caesar recalled him.

As a man he was a coward, afraid of the mob and
afraid of the censure of Tiberius, afraid of committing
an injustice and afraid to do justice. He tried theatrics
(washing his hands) and stratagem (sending Jesus to
Herod). He tried cynicism: "What *is* truth?" He knew
what truth was. He was afraid of that, too.

Maybe he died by suicide, maybe conscience killed
him. Anatole France pictures him in old age, being
asked a question about Jesus: "Jesus? Jesus? Jesus
Christ? I don't remember the name."

That's more like it. That means he was dead long before his frame collapsed. Men like Pilate *do* die like
that. "Cowards die many deaths, the valiant but once."

*Matt. 27:24; Luke 13:1; 23:1 ff.; John 18:38.*

# *Claudia Procula*

"CAESAR'S WIFE MUST BE ABOVE SUSPICION." CLAUDIA, wife of Pilate, took that old Roman proverb so to heart that she became less suspicious than Pilate.

She had the step and stature of a queen; she was of the Gens Claudia of Rome, higher in a social rank than any other woman in Palestine. Cultured and steeped in the rituals of the cold old Latin religions, the very sight of this Jesus, wearing his red badge of courage so tranquilly in the face of death, got hold of her. She could not work, or play, or sleep. That bleeding face, those unexcited eyes. . . . "Have thou nothing to do with that just man," she begged of Pilate, "for I have suffered many things this day in a dream because of him." A pagan, dreaming. A cultured pagan entering the only plea for mercy for Jesus Christ, the lowly Jew! The first Roman noblewoman to believe in Christ! What came of it? Where did Claudia Procula go from there? To far-following discipleship with Christ or to forgetfulness with Pontius?

The Greek Church reveres her as a saint. Score one for the Greek Church!

*Matthew 27:19.*

# *Barabbas*

BARABBAS, THE BRIGAND, SHOOK HIS CHAINS. HE RUBBED
his chafed ankles and stroked the palms of his hands.
Tomorrow Roman nails would pierce those hands.
Barabbas had been caught red-handed at rebellion, and
he had to die. His cross was ready. He shook his chains
and cursed his luck.

His door flew open and light streamed in. "Come out
of it, Barabbas; you're free! Jesus of Nazareth will die
in your place." They struck off the manacles; they led
him up to the prison door and turned him loose in the
sunny street. He walked off, blinking, afraid to laugh,
afraid to cry. He never knew quite what to make of it.

Neither do we. We shall never understand the sacrifice of Calvary any more than we shall understand the
incomprehensible mercy of God. All we know is that
Jesus died and that we are free. We who are guilty as
Barabbas in rebelling against our God must go on stum-
bling, blinking, in the dazzling light of that amazing
fact. It is too much for us, as it was too much for him.

*Matthew 27:15 ff.; Mark 15:6 ff.; John 18:39 f.*

# Simon of Cyrene

THE CROSS WAS LOADED ON THE SAVIOUR'S BACK, AND the hideous march began. Down to the city gates he carried it, and there, exhausted, he fell. Out of the hooting crowd the soldiers pulled a yokel, a farmer from Cyrene, Simon by name, in town to keep the Passover. "Carry it," said the centurion. Simon swung it to his shoulders. He knew how. He laid it down quickly at the top of Golgotha, and melted into the crowd again. Had there been time or chance, Jesus would have blessed him. It was the one kind deed done for him that day, done by a total stranger, a non-Jerusalemite.

The followers of Basilides (second century) said Simon was crucified instead of Christ. Unlikely. Two of his sons, Alexander and Rufus, became leaders in the Roman Church; let's think of Simon as the father of Roman Christianity.

Even had he never done more than carry that Cross, he had done enough. "Carry it!" Can you *see* him carrying it? Carry it! The call still comes as Christ is crucified afresh with each new hour, but . . . Cyrenians are scarce!

*Mark 15:21; Luke 23:26; Romans 16:13.*

# Joseph of Arimathea

THREE HEADS DROPPED ON THREE SPENT BREASTS; THE thieves and Jesus were dead. The potter's field claimed the corpses of the malefactors, but a member of the Sanhedrin claimed the body of Jesus Christ. Joseph of Arimathea, rich and just, who had failed to aid Christ at the trial, now came boldly up to Pilate and "begged the body." He got it. Pilate was glad to be rid of it.

Then Joseph took a fine linen sheet and went up the Hill of the Skull. Nicodemus met him. They drew out the nails, lowered the body, prepared it for burial. With torches flaring and the women wailing, they carried it down to Joseph's garden, laid it in a tomb prepared for Joseph's own body. Then they put out their torches and went home.

Joseph is legend's creature after that. One says he joined the seventy; another, that he took the Holy Grail to England. May the legends be verified! May just Joseph be really just! May his later faith and works give him a seat in glory with Bors, Percival and Galahad, the pure in heart who looked upon his Grail.

*Mark 15:42 ff.; Matthew 27:57 ff.; Luke 23:50 ff.;*
*John 19:38 ff.*

# *Luke*

LUKE WAS A DOCTOR AND A GENTILE. HE MAY ONCE have been a slave; slaves were often physicians. He came from Antioch. He met Paul at Troas and became his personal physician and missionary companion. A scientist and a theologian, globe-trotting for God! Science and religion joining hands, casting their nets to snare men for Christ. Two kindred, cultured, brilliant minds with but a single thought—to save a sick world in the name of the Great Physician. They followed the long trail together, came down to the end of the road where Paul cried out, "Only Luke is with me!"

He gave us the Third Gospel and parts of Acts. He gave Paul admiration and affection, professional care and personal faithfulness. He missed seeing Jesus; he came too late to travel with the Band. But when he slipped across death's gulf to be with Paul again, he surely heard the Master say, "Well done. . . . Inasmuch as ye have done it unto one of the least of these . . . ye have done it unto me."

A good doctor, Luke. He faced storm, heat, cold, eril, death itself to tend the sick. The first medical missionary!

*Acts 16:8 ff.; Col. 4:14; Philemon 24;*
*II Timothy 4:11.*

# Matthias

THE DEATH OF JUDAS LEFT A GAP IN THE DISCIPLES'
ranks, a gap that needed to be filled quickly. For a while
the Band waited for the "promise of the Father, the
baptism of the Spirit," for God to name the man; for a
while, but not for long. Then they took matters into
their own hands, nominated and elected Matthias, by a
close ballot. Politics!

There were hard feelings, jealousies over that. Matthias enjoyed no one hundred per cent popularity. As a disciple he did well enough, as well as any. He preached
well, died a martyr. Once he said, "Wonder at the
things before you." That shows he was looking in the
right direction, anyway—ahead, to the New Day. But
he was in a bad spot. He was in the position of a minister sent to a church which did not want him.

God Himself, if we may be frank, overruled the elec-
tion, putting Matthias aside to make room for a Pharisee from Tarsus. Paul was the man who really filled the
gap left by dead Judas.

Matthias must have found it hard to preach!

*Acts 1:15 ff.*

228

# *Barnabas*

THAT WAS NOT HIS NAME. "BARNABAS" WAS A DESIGNA-
tion of endearment, meaning "son of comfort." He traveled with Paul. Paul liked him; he could preach. The
people of the church liked him, he gave to the poor till
it hurt. The first thing recorded of him is that he sold his
farm and gave the sale-price to the church. "Son of
comfort," and no mistake.

When he started out with Paul (with his nephew,
Mark, in tow), Barnabas seemed the best of the three.
It was "Barnabas and Paul are doing this . . . or that."
But ere long Paul asserted himself, and folks said, "Paul
and Barnabas are . . ." Finally it was only "Paul is . . ."
They had quarreled; over John Mark, over circumci-
sion. They parted. Paul went on alone. Barnabas "sailed
away unto Cyprus" with cousin Mark.

Sad but true: family troubles and petty policies have
wrecked more than one church, more than one missionary tour. Generals *do* quarrel on the eve of battle. Years
later, they wonder why. Paul wondered why. Years
after, he spoke affectionately of Barnabas. And John
Mark came back to Paul! Barnabas had a hand in that.

Life is too short for quarrels. There is too much to be
done.

*Acts 4:36 f.; 9:27; 11:22 ff.; 14:12; 15:36 ff.;
Galatians 2:13 ff.; II Timothy 4:11.*

# Ananias

Ananias, like Barnabas, had some land. He sold it, too. He brought in a bagful of coins and said in effect to Peter: "There you are. That's *all* of it. I give it all to the church." He lied, and Peter knew it. All his blasting fury broke on Ananias' head: "Thou hast not lied unto men, but unto God."

Why did Ananias even try it? Nobody asked him to sell his land, to give a cent. Whatever Communism there was in the Apostolic Church (and there was not much) was purely voluntary. The king of liars might have kept all his coin and been asked no questions. But no—Ananias wanted his neighbors to think him a holy man; he would pad his own pocket, swindle men and bluff God from behind a camouflage of sweet charity and church.

He dealt a blow to brotherhood; he drove another spear in Jesus' side. His modern progeny are at it still. The Church has more to fear from Ananias within than from Satan without.

And ponder this. All our Utopias up to date have been thwarted by one vice, and only one—innate human selfishness.

# *Stephen*

HE HAD THE FACE AND HEART OF A BOY, THE TEMPER of a martyr begging the stake, the uncontrolled zeal of fire in tumbleweed. Stephen was the first Christian ecclesiastic, a "deacon," a distributor of alms, the first Christian martyr (who can imagine Stephen dying in bed?), and the forerunner of Paul.

Dole-handling never held him; he had to preach. And preach he did, with such convincing fury that he was haled to court. He was his own attorney. His defense was too good; it told too much truth. When Stephen flared back at his judges, calling them "stiff-necked and uncircumcised," he asked for his own death. They stoned him to death.

Young Stephen died like young Christ. It was Calvary restaged; at the end he asked that his murderers be forgiven, for they knew not what they did.

His blood was the seed of a world-encompassing Church. Because he was stoned, the disciples were dispersed; they spread the gospel around the earth. Because he was stoned, young persecutor Saul, who watched it, went off wondering, thinking, walking blindly into Jesus on the Damascus road.

*Acts 6:1-8:4.*

# Gamaliel

HERE IS HILLEL'S GRANDSON, GAMALIEL, A CREDIT INdeed to the "Old Babylonian." He knew the Law as few of his contemporaries knew it, and he did things with it they never dared to do.

From his grandfather's seat on the Sanhedrin, Gamaliel emphasized the human side of the Law, attacked its ancient rigidity with tolerance and common sense; he relaxed the childish rigor of Sabbath observance, adjusted the divorce laws to give the helpless woman a fair deal, advocated understanding instead of bigotry in the treatment of foreigners.

His classic plea for tolerance came in defense of the persecuted Apostles: "Let them alone," he advised his Sanhedrinists; "If this work be of men, it will come to naught: but if it be of God, ye cannot overthrow it."

Can we believe it? This man on the Sanhedrin of A.D. 25? A mind like this in Pilate's Jerusalem? He was a thousand years ahead of his age; thousands of our learned "doctors" have not yet caught with Gamaliel.

He was tutor to a lad from Tarsus. Young Paul sat at his feet, drinking in tolerance, breadth, depth, scholarship.

*Acts 5:34 ff.; 22:3.*

# *Paul*

~~~~~~~~~~~~~~~~~~~~~~~~~~~~~~~~~~~~~

PAUL PULLED IN THE POLES OF HIS ANCIENT WORLD AND
bound them to the Cross. From Italy to Syria he blazed
the trail for Christ. In Macedonia, Thrace, Greece, Asia
Minor, Galatia, and Pisidia; in Bithynia, Pontus, Cap-
padocia, Cilicia, Syria, Cyprus, and Idumea he threw
open to the Gentiles the doors of the Christian Church
and bade them "Come in." Along that trail the Grand
Old Missionary was whipped, stoned, starved, frozen,
shipwrecked, half drowned, and finally beheaded. None
of these things could clip his wings; his life, he knew,
was safe; union with Christ was his eternal security.

He wrote with frenzied pen; his letters now are Bible
Books, wellsprings of doctrine, the scaffolding of church
theology. Peter's spirit may be the Church's rock; Paul's
writings are the superstructure, the side walls and the
roof.

Self-sacrifice was his life's law, Calvary its passion.
Paul taught principles rather than rules; he was as courageous as he was faithful, as indifferent to criticism as
he was stubborn for righteousness. He is one of truth's
dominant heroes, Christianity's noblest martyr, the New
Testament's Moses, the pivotal portrait in the gallery of
the Soldiers of the Cross.

*I Corinthians 15:10; Romans 1:16; II Corin-
thians 11:23 ff.; Galatians 6:14; Philippians
1:21; II Timothy 4:7 f.*

# *Dorcas*

PETER WAS PREACHING AT LYDDA. TWO MEN FROM Joppa sought him out and told him Dorcas was dead. Dorcas! Peter knew Dorcas. Everyone in Lydda and Joppa knew Dorcas. She was dressmaker to the poor; she had made and fitted coats, dresses, and baby-clothes for years. Dorcas dead? That couldn't be. God wouldn't . . .

But God had. Dorcas *was* dead. Peter found her body lying in state in her Joppa house, surrounded by her widows and orphans. He sent them out, stretched his arms toward heaven for help in prayer; then he turned to the still white face and cried, "Dorcas, arise." She arose. Many, when they heard of it, believed in the Lord.

Many believed in the Lord, too, while Dorcas lived and sewed. Many looked at her and said, "If all the Christians were like that—!" Her needle was a missionary.

"Dorcas societies" were widespread in the churches of the last generation; in ours they are nearly gone. But Dorcas is not dead. She cannot die. God wouldn't . . . We see Him in the lives of the Dorcas-minded; we touch His very hands as we touch the hands of those who help.

*Acts 9:36 ff.*

# Silas

"SUBSTITUTES ARE NEVER JUST AS GOOD." OH YES, THEY are. Sometimes even better than the originals. The "regulars" may be the first to go to war, but it often takes the raw volunteer to win it!

Silas was a substitute. He volunteered to go with Paul when Barnabas broke ranks. Paul knew him well and quickly accepted him. Bold, liberal, leading Jewish Christian and Roman citizen, he was made for the perils of the road. Off he went, through South Galatia, to Troas and Philippi, to Thessalonica, Berea, and Corinth. He preached with his beloved superior in the face of violence and enmity, faced mobs by day and stealthy death by night.

They were bound to stakes together and scourged in the marketplace, were chained together in a Philippian jail. The stripes they accepted as God's chevrons, the chains made them so happy that they sang through the prison night.

Substitute, was he, or regular? Baring his back to the whip because a friend was baring his, laying down his life for a Friend he had never seen, yet loved? Silas was ultra-regular.

*Acts 15:22 ff.; 16:25 ff.; I Thessalonians 1:1;*
*II Corinthians 1:19; I Peter 5:12.*

# Timothy

TIMOTHY, TOO, WAS A SUBSTITUTE. HE STEPPED IN when Mark stepped out, saying, "Send me." His mother was Jewish, his father Greek. Great combination. Likely, he had the face of a Chopin, the fingers of a Michelangelo. His was not the robustness of a Silas at the whipping-post, but the strength of a rose folding 'gainst the rain.

Not that persecution dodged him. He met plenty of it, and he wore well. He was Paul's cell companion; more than once he felt death's breath upon his cheek.

Paul used him as a courier, running messages hither and yon. He trusted Timothy with precious parchment and bags of coin, and with the ruling of the church at Ephesus.

One day a solemn summons came to Timothy. Paul, in prison, knew death was close. "Come . . . take Mark, and bring him with thee." In the last hours they sat together, grizzled veteran and young volunteer. From failing hand to strong one passed the torch; then, supported by those Michelangelo hands, the old warrior waited for time to sound "Taps."

Or was it for God to sound "Reveille"?

*Acts 16:1 ff.; 17:14 ff.; I Thessalonians 3:1 ff.;*
*I Corinthians 4:17; Colossians 1:1; Philemon*
*2:19; I Timothy 1:3 ff.; II Timothy 4:19 ff.*

# Lydia

THE SWAGGER OF SUCCESS WAS IN HER WALK. LYDIA was a business woman, alert, ambitious, traveled, progressive, successful in an age when men were merchants and women underlings. A seller of purple in Philippi, she traded with men on even terms and beat the best of them in many a close deal.

Pual and Silas had come to Philippi to hold a singing prayer-meeting at the riverside. Among their auditors was Lydia, the merchant; among their converts was Lydia, the devout. Social criticism? She laughed at it. Effect on her business? She never thought of that. Lydia put first things first. Christ first, then business. "Come to my house," she bade the missionaries; her home, thereafter, was an asylum for the wanderers of the Cross. Lydia was the first home missionary, the hostess of the first cottage prayer-meeting.

Sellers of purple in New York say Christ and purple will not mix. Why? Is there something wrong with Christ—or with business? And have they tried it? Dare they try it? Have they the courage—and the forward look—of hostess Lydia?

*Acts 16:14 f.*

# *Dionysius*

LAUGHTER AND RIDICULE ARE MEANER WEAPONS THAN
fagot and rope. Martyrdom lends dignity to any cause;
well-aimed raillery will kill it. The Athenians threw no
stones when Paul came preaching to their town; they
only laughed at him. It baffled him. He wandered for-
lornly about their streets, knowing not where to cast his
seeds. Athens was stony ground. No field for him here.
He shook the dust of the city from his feet and made
for Corinth.

He always thought that he had failed at Athens, that
here was his great defeat. He had not failed. Dionysius
the Areopagite (sixty years old, man of position,
member of the University council of Athens) heard and
believed. Eusebius claims that Dionysius became the
first Bishop of Athens, and that he was martyred.

That's the joy of preaching. The preacher never
knows! He scatters his seed, and generations later,
when he is dead, a flower comes to bloom. Bishop Tay-
lor labored seven years in India for his first man. A
Scotch country parson gave his life to one parish and
led just one boy to the altar. But the boy's name was
David Livingstone.

*Acts 17:16 ff.; 34.*

# Priscilla

SHE AND HER HUSBAND, AQUILA, MADE TENTS. THEY
had tent habits; never drove their stakes very deep, but
kept moving. Their tent flap was never tied shut. Their
home was a rendezvous for Christians, a hotel for missionaries.

Driven from Rome by edict of Claudius, they sewed
tents for a while in Corinth. Paul visited them there,
perhaps stitched a few seams (Paul knew how), and
preached a few sermons. They were together again at
Ephesus, and yet again at Rome. Their household became famous; their friends received letters from them
which began, "Aquila and Priscilla salute you much in
the Lord, with the church that is in their home."

Tradition has been good to Priscilla, giving her a
church (St. Prisca's, on Rome's Aventine), a book, the
*Acts of St. Prisca,* and crediting her with the author-
ship of the Epistle to the Hebrews! Let tradition have
all that. Let us have Priscilla calling Christians into the
shelter of her house when others were losing their heads
for doing less, a woman who rejoiced to preach the glad
tidings at whatever cost.

*Acts 18:1 ff.; I Corinthians 16, 19; Romans 16,
3; II Timothy 4. 19.*

# Diana

GREAT WAS DIANA (REALLY, ARTEMIS) OF THE EPHE-
sians. Great in carnality, conspicuous for her lack of
chastity, her revels in lechery. She is the New Testament Astarte.

She was an Anatolian deity, many-breasted, a wan-
derer worshiped over the whole of Lydia. Her rude
idol-likeness in her central temple at Ephesus, men said,
had fallen from heaven. She fell farther than that, and
dragged half the world down with her.

Paul had a hard time of it in Ephesus. Diana had
been there long before the Greeks; for generations
Ephesians had been rolling in a moral mud bath. Feed a
people for even a week on a Diana diet, and you may
expect almost anything.

Diana is no more; her world has been washed clean
in the blood of the Lamb. A few may still kneel to her
in spirit, but they are very few. Christ's Cross has always been morality's broom. Wherever he appears,
Diana flees and morality moves up another step toward
perfect purity.

*Acts 19:24 ff.*

# Demetrius

COMPLETELY COMMERCIALIZED, DIANA WAS SOLD IN images of marble and terra-cotta to the poor, in silver to the rich. The image trade was the most profitable in Ephesus; every house had her suggestive statue in the parlor—had one, two, three, four of them. Demetrius put them on the mantelpieces of the rich; he was a silversmith.

Came Paul, turning men's eyes from mute Diana in silver to the risen, wonder-working Christ; came a fall, therefore, in the profits of the image-makers. Demetrius called a meeting of the silver men and made a speech: "Sirs, ye know that by this craft we have our wealth." It was the spark to the powder; the town blew up to riot.

Pinch a man's pride or faith or sense and he will not fight hard; pinch his pocketbook and he squeals like a bleeding pig. Preachers denouncing child labor or the bloody traffic of alcohol or armaments are asked, "Sirs, know ye not that by our craft we have our wealth?"

Paul and Demetrius, like two antler-locked stags, are still fighting it out.

*Acts 19:23 ff.*

# *Felix*

PROCURATOR FELIX, OF JUDEA, WAS BROTHER IN SPIRIT to Pontius Pilate, brother in flesh to Pallas, the influential freedman of Claudius. He had need of Pallas; this friend at Court kept him in office in spite of his very bad administration as governor, and saved his life in his final disgrace.

Felix might have set Paul free; his was the power. But set him free he would not. He held him first in hope of a bribe (Paul was socially important), and then in fear of the Jews. For two years he held the Apostle in chains; for two years he was more tortured than Paul. For Paul preached to Felix, every time chance offered, of righteousness and temperance and the Judgment Day! Felix writhed and trembled, but cupidity overcame his fears.

Who can understand such men? Whatever is it within them that makes them postpone making right decision, holding out for a paltry bribe while God and conscience drag them through the fires of hell?

*Acts 23:24 ff.; 24:1 ff.*

# *Festus*

GOD'S WAYS, AND FATE'S, ARE SOMETIMES STRANGE; tyrants live long and the good die young. Festus was a better procurator than Felix, but his reign was only three years long. Paul respected him, called him "most noble Festus," and meant it.

He had more spine than Felix; he refused to surrender Paul to the Jews without fair trial. But he could not be trusted far. Festus was a politician, a diplomat, a compromiser. "Wilt thou go up to Jerusalem, and there be judged?" he asked the prisoner. It was a trick. Something of a lawyer himself, Paul took the breath from Festus with a demand that he be tried not by Jerusalem, but Rome! "I appeal unto Caesar." Festus could do nothing but let him go, for Paul was a citizen of Rome.

With Pilate and Felix, he had missed his chance; he is neither great nor little to us, but mediocre. Like most compromisers, his record is not worth writing down. He might have been the noblest Roman of the three; he is only a . . . politician.

*Acts 25-26.*

# Agrippa

A ROYAL STRANGER SAT WITH FESTUS IN THE COURT.
Agrippa, King Marcus Julius Agrippa II, a Herod, had
come on an official visit to Cesarea. Festus told him of
Paul. "I would also hear the man myself," said Agrippa.
A king's whim is a subordinate's command; next day
Paul faced him.

Paul did well before him, so well that the king's curi-
osity gave way to conviction. He listened to Paul's story
of his life as Pharisee and Christian, heard him say
proudly, as he stood there in chains, "I was not disobe-
dient unto the heavenly vision." He saw immediately
that here was no criminal, no blasphemer, no candidate
for headsman's ax. "Almost," he said to Paul as he ad-
journed the court—"almost thou persuadest me to be a
Christian."

Agrippa was more than almost persuaded; convinced
against his will, he took refuge behind a shabbily trans-
parent screen of irony. After all, Agrippa must remember his position. He was a king! A king could not
run with this rabble of Nazarenes. He dismissed the
matter with a lawyer's subterfuge: "This man might
have been set at liberty if he had not appealed unto
Caesar."

But how did that help you, Agrippa?

*Acts 25:13-26:32.*

# *Phoebe*

MEN ALONE HAVE NEVER WON A WAR; WOMEN HAVE
helped. Men alone, in the first-century church, could
never have won their fight for Christ. Their women received little notice, little applause (Paul himself told
them to "keep silence in the churches"), but their work
was invaluable, just the same. Paul realized that. "I
commend unto you Phoebe, our sister," he writes to the
Romans, "for she hath been a succorer of many, and of
myself also."

Phoebe was a Deaconess, a European Greek, known
to Paul for her labors at Corinth. He does not say what
those labors were, what was the nature of her succoring.
Did she play hostess, like Lydia, to missionaries? Or
spend her time teaching, visiting the poor, nursing?

Paul found her dependable in whatever she did. He
trusted her once with a most important errand. At the
end of his Epistle to the Romans you will find a post-
script, reading, "Written to the Romans from
Corinthus, and sent by Phoebe, servant of the church at
Cenchrea."

It is claimed in some quarters that Deaconess Phoebe
even wrote that letter herself!

*Romans 16:1 f.*

# *Chloe*

SOME ONE IN HER HOUSE TALKED OUT OF TURN; SOME of "them which are of the house of Chloe" carried a sad tale to Paul, told him confidently that all was not well in Chloe's Corinth. There had come dissensions; the church was splitting up. Some of the brethren were saying that they were "of Paul," others that they were of Apollos, or Cephas, or Christ.

Paul wrote a blistering letter to Corinth: "Is Christ divided? Were ye baptized in the name of Paul? . . . I thank God that I baptized none of you, but Crispus and Gaius."

Chloe herself may have been a Christian or a heathen; those informers from her house may have been either her Christian slaves or her close friends. That means nothing. What matters here is that from her home came the first rumors of Christian denominationalism.

Her informers would be busy today. We have but one Christ . . . and more than two hundred Protestant denominations. We have but one God . . . and ten thousand doctrines. We have need of but one baptism . . . but we have immersion, sprinkling, pouring. Our most familiar hymn is,

> Onward, Christian soldiers,
> All one body, we!

One body? Not yet!

*1 Corinthians 1:11, 13.*

# *Titus*

"Mine own son after the common faith," Paul called him. They had much in common. Both had patience, prudence, tact, determination, brains. Once they missed an appointment. "I had no rest in my spirit," said Paul, "because I found not Titus."

He was Greek, the first uncircumcised Christian. Paul took him down to Jerusalem as a test case for the council which settled the circumcision controversy. Paul won; thereafter the Greek convert was known abroad as the leader of the church of the uncircumcision.

Titus went on two great assignments. Thrice he was sent to Corinth to lay down the law on immorality (the Corinthians were backsliding) and to take a collection for the poor. Later he worked with Paul in Crete, where all men were "liars, evil beasts, slow bellies [gluttons]." He plucked thistles and planted flowers in Crete. The Cretans liked him and elected him their first bishop.

Messenger, test case, bishop—that was good. Better than that is this: Titus shared with Timothy the honor of being Paul's most efficient helper. The Greek and the Jew needed one another as the artery needs a heart, or the heart the artery.

*Titus 1:4, 12; II Corinthians 2:13; 7:8; 8:16 ff.;*
*Acts 15:24 ff.; Galatians 2:3 ff.*

# *Demas*

"DEMAS HATH FORSAKEN ME, HAVING LOVED THIS PRES-
ent world," writes Paul to Timothy. Demas quit. Over
his vacant niche in the Apostolic Hall of Fame the muse
of history has carved one awful word: "Deserter." He
was not the only one; he was the worst.

Barnabas deserted because he disagreed; he went on
working elsewhere. Others were lured off the main highway by false teachers; they were sincere. But Demas
just quit. This world was too much with him; the next
too far away. He had suffered prison, denial, depriva-
tion for the sake of an invisible Kingdom; he was tired
of it. He wanted a little ease before he died, a house, a
jug of wine, a loaf. A man might get that out of this
world, this present world, before death came. "One
world at a time," said Demas, and "good-by."

He overlooked something: This world is quite what
we make it; there are many mansions in it; yours may
be ramshackle or beautiful, as you will. And the two
worlds are not separated; the invisible dwells within the
visible; they are one.

Demas hath forsaken *me?* No, Demas hath forsaken
Demas.

*Colossians 4:14; Philemon 24; II Timothy 4:10.*

248

# *Philetus*

"THEIR WORD WILL EAT AS DOTH A CANKER," SAID PAUL of Hymeneus and Philetus. He was worried over their influence on the church. They were talking wildly about the resurrection. They had a new idea about all that. For them it was to be spoken of in the past tense; it was over and done. They understood it to be a "rising from sin to holiness"; there was to be no resurrection of any body, no life to come. Thus they swept away in an instant a hope which had held mankind since the dawn of the first day.

Philetus fights the universe; the stars in their courses stand against him. Nothing ever dies. All things change. Ask any good scientist, biologist, anthropologist. Life changes, but it goes on; the fine red thread of eternity runs through its core.

No, Philetus, the earth is not the end, but only a training-school. God has a better use for men than they yet know of; he does not plague us, make us struggle for threescore years and ten and then drop us in a grave. He is preparing us.

*II Timothy 2:17 f.*

# *Onesimus*

ONESIMUS WAS A SLAVE; HE RAN AWAY. PAUL FOUND him and sent him back to his master, Philemon. "Receive him," he asked the master, ". . . not now as a servant, but above a servant, a brother. . . . If he has wronged thee . . . or oweth thee . . . put that on mine account!"

One Aurelius Sarapammon, says an old papyri, also lost a slave at about this time. "Shut him up, whip him, lay a complaint before the authorities," he writes to a friend. The difference between Aurelius and Paul is the difference between a man who knows Christ and a man who does not; the difference in their worlds is the difference between the worlds before Christ came into it, and after. Christ drove slavery from the earth, destroyed both masters and slaves, made them brothers.

So we end the portrait-gallery of the Book with Onesimus the slave, trudging homeward from one who was proud to be called the "prisoner of Christ," to one who was no longer his master but his fellow servant in Christ, in the name of one who boasted, "I am among you as he that serveth."

*Philemon 10 ff.*